A Concise
User's Guide
to MS-DOS 5

by

Noel Kantaris

BERNARD BABANI (publishing) LTD.
THE GRAMPIANS
SHEPHERDS BUSH ROAD
LONDON W6 7NF
ENGLAND

PLEASE NOTE

Although every care has been taken with the production of this book to ensure that any projects, designs, modifications and/or programs, etc., contained herewith, operate in a correct and safe manner and also that any components specified are normally available in Great Britain, the Publishers and Author(s) do not accept responsibility in any way for the failure (including fault in design) of any project, design, modification or program to work correctly or to cause damage to any equipment that it may be connected to or used in conjunction with, or in respect of any other damage or injury that may be so caused, nor do the Publishers accept responsibility in any way for the failure to obtain specified components.

Notice is also given that if equipment that is still under warranty is modified in any way or used or connected with home-built equipment then that warranty may be void.

© 1992 BERNARD BABANI (pub.) LTD

First Published — April 1992
Reprinted — February 1993

British Library Cataloguing in Publication Data:

Kantaris, Noel
   Concise User's Guide to MS-DOS 5
   I. Title
   005.44

ISBN 0 85934 318 9

Printed and Bound in Great Britain by Cox & Wyman Ltd, Reading

A Concise User's Guide to MS-DOS 5

ALSO AVAILABLE

(By the same author)

BP232 A Concise Introduction to MS-DOS

BP243 BBC-BASIC86 on Amstrad PCs & IBM Compatibles
       Book 1 - Language

BP244 BBC-BASIC86 on Amstrad PCs & IBM Compatibles
       Book 2 - Graphics and Disk Files

BP250 Programming in FORTRAN 77

BP258 Learning to Program in C

BP259 A Concise Introduction to UNIX

BP260 A Concise Introduction to OS/2

BP264 A Concise Advanced User's Guide to MS-DOS

BP274 A Concise Introduction to SuperCalc5

BP270 A Concise Introduction to Symphony

BP279 A Concise Introduction to Excel

BP283 A Concise Introduction to SmartWare II

BP284 Programming in QuickBASIC

BP288 A Concise Introduction to Windows 3.0

BP294 A Concise Introduction to Microsoft Works

BP302 A Concise User's Guide to Lotus 1-2-3 Release 3.1

BP314 A Concise Introduction to Quattro Pro 3.0

ABOUT THIS BOOK

To help the beginner, this concise guide to MS-DOS 5, has been written with an underlying structure based on 'what you need to know first, appears first'. However, the book is also circular, which means that you don't have to start at the beginning and go to the end. The more experienced user can start from any section, as each section has been designed to be self contained.

This book does not seek to replace the documentation you receive with the MS-DOS 5 operating system, but only to supplement and explain it. The book covers systems with both hard disc-based drives, and floppy disc-based drives as applicable to the PC, and compatible microcomputers.

The book deals with the enhancements to be found in the MS-DOS version 5, one aspect of which is substantially different to earlier versions of the operating system. This is due to the refinement of the DOS shell, a menu-driven graphical interface, which first appeared in version 4.0. The menus employed in the DOS shell are consistent with those used in Microsoft Windows (prior to version 3.0) which should make it easier to use.

This book was written with the busy person in mind. You don't need to read hundreds of pages to find out most that there is to know about the subject, when a few pages can do the same thing quite adequately! Naturally, selectivity of subject matter is of paramount importance, so that the reader does not miss vital points. In particular, the book seeks to bring to the forefront and exploit the inherent simplicity in the MS-DOS operating system by presenting, with examples, the principles of what you need to know, when you need to know them.

At the same time, the book has been written in such a way as to also act as a reference guide, long after you have mastered most MS-DOS commands. To this end, a summary of the commands supported by the MS-DOS operating system is given in the penultimate section of this book. The commands are explained with relevant examples and, as such, the section can serve as a quick reference guide.

ABOUT THE AUTHOR

Graduated in Electrical Engineering at Bristol University and after spending three years in the Electronics Industry in London, took up a Tutorship in Physics at the University of Queensland. Research interests in Ionospheric Physics, led to the degrees of M.E. in Electronics and Ph.D. in Physics. On return to the UK, he took up a Post-Doctoral Research Fellowship in Radio Physics at the University of Leicester, and in 1973 a Senior Lectureship in Engineering at The Camborne School of Mines, Cornwall, where since 1978 he has also assumed the responsibility of Head of Computing.

ACKNOWLEDGEMENTS

I would like to thank colleagues at the Camborne School of Mines for the helpful tips and suggestions which assisted me in the writing of this book.

ACKNOWLEDGEMENTS

TRADEMARKS

CONTENTS

1. INTRODUCTION

Most 16-bit microcomputers use Microsoft's Disc Operating System (MS-DOS) as the prime means of interaction between user and computer. Owners of IBM PCs know this operating system as PC-DOS, which is IBM's implementation of MS-DOS. The name MS-DOS or DOS will be used throughout this book to distinguish this operating system from another popular one, namely Digital Research's DR-DOS.

Versions of MS-DOS

Since its inception in 1981, MS-DOS has been the standard operating system for personal computers and by now is being used by more than 50 million people. As the number of users increased over the years, so too has the complexity of applications run on their PCs. To meet these ever increasing demands, MS-DOS has also increased its functionality several times in the form of *new* versions, as shown in the table below.

Version	Date	Main changes in functionality
1.0	1981	Original Disc Operating System
1.25	1982	Support for double-sided discs
2.0	1983	Support for sub-directories
2.25	1983	Support for extended character set
3.0	1984	Support for 1.2MB floppy disc and larger capacity hard disc
3.1	1984	Support for PC networks
3.2	1986	Support for 3½" floppy disc
3.3	1987	Support for PS/2 computer range
4.0	1988	Support for extended memory (EMS), hard disc partitions beyond 32MB, and the graphical user interface DOS shell
4.01	1989	Fix bugs in 4.0 version.
5.0	1991	Ability to run DOS in high memory and certain device drivers in upper memory, the adoption of a full screen editor and context sensitive help, and support for a 2.88MB floppy disc.

Several aspects of version 5 differ from earlier versions. For example, the addition of context sensitive help, a full screen editor, and an improved DOS shell - a menu-driven graphical interface - makes this version easier to use.

New Features in MS-DOS 5

In general, it is worth upgrading to MS-DOS 5 from any version of MS-DOS. Apart from the features listed below, you gain an advanced memory management system which leaves more memory for your DOS applications. For example, upgrading from version 3.x gives you at least 45 Kbytes of extra memory on a computer with Intel's 80286 or higher processor, while upgrading, on a comparable computer, from version 4.01 gives you at least 55 Kbytes of extra memory. The memory management of MS-DOS 5 and the advantages gained by its use, will be discussed shortly under a separate section.

Other new features to be found in MS-DOS 5, include the following:

- Ease of learning with the new DOS Shell, an improved GUI (Graphical User Interface) which allows you to manage programs and switch between them, view the directory structure of any disc, and view the contents of several directories at the same time.

- On-line, context sensitive help. To obtain help, simply type the MS-DOS command followed by /?, or type **help** followed by the MS-DOS command.

- A full screen editor which replaces the famous **edlin** line editor.

- The ability of create and maintain large disc partitions (without the need of running the SHARE program, as was the case with MS-DOS version 4.x).

- The ability to search for files through multiple levels of directories.

- The ability to sort directory listings by filename, type of file, the date and time of file creation, and size of file.

- The addition of DOSKEY, a program that allows you to recall, edit and execute already used commands.

- The inclusion of QBasic, an improved Basic programming environment which replaces GWBasic.

- The ability to access more than two hard disc drives.

- The support for the new 2.88 Mbyte floppy discs.

Installing MS-DOS 5

MS-DOS 5 comes in two formats; an upgrade set of discs which allows you to upgrade to version 5 from previous versions of DOS without having to reformat your hard disc, and a set of discs which allow you to configure a brand new system. What steps you take when you first start, depend on which format of MS-DOS 5 you are trying to install. If you are upgrading your operating system from an existing version to MS-DOS 5 skip to the next section.

If you are installing MS-DOS 5 to a new system, insert Disc #1 of the distribution discs in the A: drive, and switch on the power to your computer (it is assumed, of course, that you are familiar with handling floppy discs, floppy and hard disc drives, and that the installation manual which comes with the operating system has been read). This will cause MS-DOS to be loaded from the A: drive and start the SETUP program automatically. From there on, just follow the instructions appearing on the screen. Soon, SETUP will inform you that the new operating system was installed successfully.

The MS-DOS operating system consists of a collection of small, specialised programs that make up the working environment which allows you to create and save programs, copy or delete data files from disc or perform other input and output (I/O) operations, such as finding a program or a file on a particular disc or sending the contents of that file to the printer.

In general, MS-DOS is the micro's administrator and understanding the way it works is very important. Running a computer without understanding its operating system is similar to trying to run a library without any knowledge of librarianship; very soon chaos will be the order of the day.

If you have installed MS-DOS 5 to a new system, you can skip the next section which is only relevant to those who are upgrading from an existing MS-DOS version.

Upgrading to MS-DOS 5

With the upgrade version of MS-DOS 5, you will have to start your computer in the normal way, then insert Disc #1 of the distribution discs in drive A:, type A: at the prompt to log to the A: drive, then type SETUP to start the installation program.

On starting, SETUP informs you that your original MS-DOS files will be upgraded to MS-DOS 5, but that you will need a

newly formatted disc (or more, depending on available size) to
be able to restore the original DOS to your hard disc later, if
needed, by displaying the following screen:

```
Microsoft(R) MS-DOS(R) Version 5.00
_____

        Welcome to Setup

        Setup upgrades your original DOS files to MS-DOS version 5.0.
        During Setup you need to provide a floppy disk (or disks).
        Setup will use the disk(s) to store your original DOS files.
        Label the disk(s) as follows.

           UNINSTALL #1
           UNINSTALL #2 (if needed)

        The disk(s), which can be unformatted or newly formatted,
        must be used in drive A:.

        Setup copies some files to the Uninstall disk(s), and
        others to a directory on your hard disk called OLD_DOS.x.
        Using these files, you can restore the original DOS on your
        hard disk if you need to.


ENTER=Continue  F1=Help  F3=Exit  F5=Remove Color
```

SETUP then offers you the opportunity of backing up your hard
disc. If you haven't done so already, now is your last chance to
avoid possible disaster. Next, SETUP finds out the hardware
configuration of your system. In my case, it displayed the
following information:

```
Microsoft(R) MS-DOS(R) Version 5.00
_____

        Setup has determined that your system includes the
        following hardware and software components.

        ┌─────────────────────────────────────────────────┐
        │ DOS Type     :TOSHIBA                             │
        │ DOS Path     :C:\DOS                              │
        │ MS-DOS Shell :Run MS-DOS Shell on startup.        │
        │ Display Type :VGA                                 │
        │ Continue Setup: The information above is correct. │
        └─────────────────────────────────────────────────┘

        If all the items in the list are correct, press ENTER.
        If you want to change an item in the list, use the UP
        ARROW or DOWN ARROW key to select it.  Then press ENTER
        to see alternatives for that item.


ENTER=Continue  F1=Help  F3=Exit
```

4

You can, of course, change any of the options offered, such as having the option of the MS-DOS Shell run on startup, by highlighting what you want to change and pressing <Enter>.

SETUP starts to install MS-DOS 5, but after 4% of the installation is completed it asks you to insert the 'Uninstall Disc #1' into the A: drive so that it can copy information to it which will be needed if you decide at a later stage to start your system with the older version of DOS. Having copied the required files, SETUP requests that you insert distribution Disc #1 back into the A: drive and continues with the upgrade. A percentage bar keeps you informed of the installation's progress and after all the distribution discs have been copied and the installation is completed, the following screen is displayed:

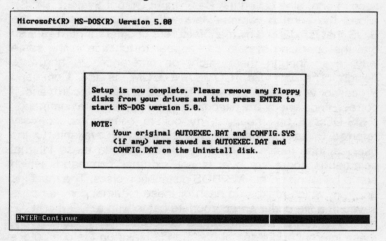

If you now look at the directory listing, you will see that your old DOS files have been moved to the OLD_DOS.1 directory. These files and the information contained in your 'Uninstall Disc' are required should you ever decide to use the old version of DOS.

Conversely, should you decide that you do not need the old version of DOS, you could delete the contents of OLD_DOS.1 and remove its sub-directory from the root directory of your hard disc. This would save you about 1.5 Mbytes of disc space which you could use to install other packages. How you can delete the contents of whole directories will be discussed later.

The Structure of MS-DOS

To understand how to use MS-DOS you must understand its underlying structure. The various DOS administrative functions are contained in three separate main files (later on we will explain what files mean and their naming convention). These are:

MSDOS.SYS
IO.SYS
COMMAND.COM

or IBMDOS.COM, IBMBIO.COM and COMMAND.COM, in the case of the IBM PC.

The first file is the core of the operating system, while the second one, also called the Basic Input Output System (BIOS), allows the core to communicate with the hardware. It is the BIOS that is adapted by manufacturers of different hardware so that the operating system can appear to function in the same way, even though there might be differences in hardware design. The last file, COMMAND.COM, is the Command Processor which analyzes what is typed at the keyboard, and if correct, finds and starts execution of the appropriate command.

MS-DOS 5 has nearly thirty built-in commands, normally referred to as 'internal commands', instantly available to the user as they reside in memory. In addition to these internal commands, there are over ninety 'external' commands which are to be found on the MS-DOS distribution discs. The machine program which makes up each of these external commands is saved in a *file* under an appropriate name with a .COM or .EXE extension to the filename (more about this later). Collectively, these internal and external commands make up the computer's Disc Operating System (DOS). These commands will be examined in detail in the following chapters of this book.

Booting up the System:

Whenever you start your computer by switching on the power, the system is booted up, which is normally indicated by the appearance of a C> or A> prompt, for booting from a hard or floppy disc drive, respectively. The word 'normally' was used here because you might be running the DOS Shell (or some other interface), in which case you will not see the usual C> prompt.

Now, displaying a listing of the directory (by typing **DIR** at the prompt and pressing <Enter>), will reveal the contents of your disc, but neither of the first two System files (MSDOS.SYS and IO.SYS) will appear on the directory list as they are hidden. Only the third file (COMMAND.COM) will be displayed.

In addition to these three special files, there are a number of other DOS files which perform various important tasks. These are collectively known as the DOS utilities and will be examined in detail later. To be able to distinguish between disc drives, MS-DOS refers to them by a letter followed by a colon, i.e. C: or A: for the prime drive of the appropriate system. In a twin floppy disc-based system, there are two drives; A: and B:, with drive A: being the leftmost or uppermost of the two, while on a hard disc-based system there is a hard disc drive, C: and a floppy disc drive, A:. DOS allows you to also refer to drive A: as drive B:, so that you can copy files from one floppy disc to another using a single floppy disc drive. Users on networked systems can access a network hard disc by assigning it as another drive on their micro, namely as E: or Z:

On booting up a microcomputer, the following tasks are performed:

- A self test on its Random Access Memory (RAM) is performed

- A check is made to see if a floppy disc is in drive A:, and if there is, whether it is a System disc. If it is, it boots the system from the A: drive

- If no floppy exists in drive A:, an attempt is made to boot the system from drive C:, if there is one, otherwise in the case of the IBM, it goes into Read Only Memory (ROM) based BASIC

- Configures the system by executing the CONFIG.SYS file

- Reads the BIOS and the MS-DOS operating system

- Loads into RAM the COMMAND.COM file so that internal commands can be made available instantly

- Executes the commands within the AUTOEXEC.BAT file, if one exists, otherwise it asks for the Date and Time which can be reset at this point. Pressing the <Enter> key, confirms what is displayed.

7

Should you receive any error message while these tasks are being performed, you could restart the process, after rectifying the error, by pressing simultaneously the three keys marked **Ctrl**, **Alt** and **Del**, shown in this book as **Ctrl+Alt+Del**. This will re-boot the system, and is referred to as a 'warm re-boot'. In contrast, re-booting the system by switching the power off and then back on again, is referred to as a 'cold re-boot'.

Internal DOS Commands

MS-DOS has nearly thirty internal commands built into it which are instantly available as they reside in memory. These are listed below:

Command	Meaning
BREAK	Sets the Ctrl+Break check on or off
CALL	Calls one batch file from another
CHCP	Displays or changes the active code page
CD or CHDIR	Change the current directory
CLS	Clears the screen
COPY	Copies files
CTTY	Changes the standard Input/Output device
DATE	Displays or sets the system date
DEL	Deletes the specified files
DIR	Displays the disc directory
ECHO	Sets Echo to on or off
EXIT	Exits to the previous command level
FOR	Repeats a command for each item in a set
GOTO	Jumps to a labelled line within the same batch file
IF	Allows conditional execution of commands within a batch file
MD or MKDIR	Makes (creates) a new directory
PATH	Searches alternative directories
PAUSE	Pauses execution of the batch file
PROMPT	Changes the system prompt
REM	Allows remarks to be added in a batch file
REN or RENAME	Renames files
RD or RMDIR	Removes (deletes) a directory
SET	Changes the system parameters
SHIFT	Allows more than 10 replaceable parameters in a batch file.
TIME	Displays or sets the system time
TYPE	Displays a specified text file
VER	Displays the MS-DOS version
VERIFY	Checks disc writing
VOL	Displays the disc volume label.

The internal DOS commands (most of which will be explained later), together with the rest of the operating system, occupy some 65 Kbytes of RAM, as they are loaded into memory on booting up the system. Where exactly in memory these commands are loaded, depends on the type of processor in your system.

Memory Management of MS-DOS 5

On computers with Intel's 80286 or higher processor, MS-DOS 5 loads itself in 'extended' memory (the memory between 1 and 16 Mbytes - or even higher on 80386 and 80486 machines), freeing at least 45 Kbytes of 'conventional' memory (the first 640 Kbytes of RAM), for your DOS applications. The extended memory (including the first 64 Kbytes above the 1 Mbyte) known as HMA - the High Memory Area, is managed by the new version of HIGHMEM.SYS, while the conventional memory is managed by a built-in memory manager using MCBs (Memory Control Blocks).

A pictorial view of how memory is managed on a typical 80286 computer when using MS-DOS 3.3, and what happens when MS-DOS 5 is used in conjunction with the **DOS=HIGH** command in the CONFIG.SYS file (more about this later), is shown below.

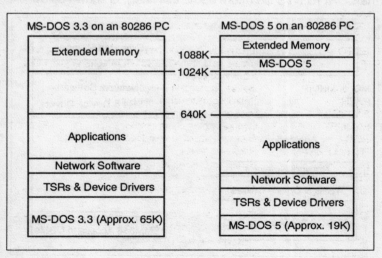

On computers with Intel's more advanced 80386 or higher processor, you can load device drivers, TSR (Terminate and Stay Resident) programs, and network software drivers into 'upper' memory (the memory between 640 Kbytes and 1024 Mbytes). The chunks of memory available to the user, between the various hardware-dependent ROMs and the video memory, is managed by UMBs (Upper Memory Blocks) and access to these is governed by the EMM386.EXE utility (previously used with Windows 3.0 to provide expanded memory), thus freeing even more space in conventional memory for DOS applications.

Unfortunately, the 32 Kbyte video ROM splits the free area in upper memory into two sections, a lower area of 32 Kbytes and a higher area of 96 Kbytes. In addition, the 64 Kbyte BIOS ROM sits in the segment just below the 1 Mbyte position. Thus, what you load in upper memory, and where (i.e. in what order), depends on the size of the files you are loading. For this reason, MS-DOS leaves this bit of fine tuning entirely to the user.

The corresponding pictorial view of how memory is managed on a typical 80386 computer when using MS-DOS 3.3, and what happens when MS-DOS 5 is used in conjunction with the **DEVICE=EMM386.EXE** and **DOS=HIGH, UMB** commands in the CONFIG.SYS file (more about this later), is shown below.

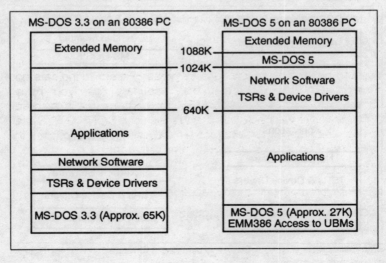

The fine tuning of loading the maximum number of device drivers into upper memory can either be done by trial and error, by finding out the size of the various blocks with the use of the **MEM /C** command and loading the required device drivers in the available memory blocks with the use of the **DEVICEHIGH=** command in the AUTOEXEC.BAT file, or with the help of a proprietary software package, such as Quarterdeck's utility QEMM386 version 6, which can even move the ROM image into extended memory, thus making more contiguous space available in upper memory.

Illustrating Internal MS-DOS Commands

As an illustration of internal MS-DOS commands, consider the two which allow you to re-set the date and time of your computer's clock. If you are running the DOS Shell, it will be necessary to select the 'Command Prompt' option from the Main menu at the lower half of the DOS Shell screen, in order to emulate what is presented below.

The DATE & TIME Commands:

Your computer is equipped with an internal clock, whose date and time can be changed. Typing the command

    C>DATE

at the C> prompt, evokes the response

    Current date is dd/mm/yy
    Enter new date:

You can either type a new date, or press <Enter> to indicate no change. The above date format assumes that you have included the command COUNTRY=xxx, where xxx is a three digit code representing your country, in your CONFIG.SYS file (to be discussed later), otherwise the date will be shown in mm/dd/yy format. Similarly, typing the command

    C>TIME

at the C> prompt, evokes the response

    Current time is Hrs:Mins:Secs
    Enter new time:

at which point you can either type a new time, or press <Enter> to indicate that time is not to be changed.

11

External DOS Commands

DOS provides over ninety additional commands which, to avoid eating up more of the computer's memory, reside on disc. These are known as external commands and can only be invoked if a disc containing the required files is accessible. In the case of a floppy disc-based system some of these files will be found on the System disc in the A: drive (DOS can be installed on floppies). For a hard disc-based system, these additional files would have been transferred onto the DOS sub-directory of the C: drive and can be accessed from it.

Files and the Disc Directory

To see a directory listing of the MS-DOS command files, type **DIR** at the A> prompt (for a floppy disc-based system) or type **DIR \DOS** at the C> prompt (for a hard disc-based system), and press <Enter>. If you are running the DOS Shell, select the DOS sub-directory (by pointing and clicking with the mouse, or pressing the <Tab> key to move to the 'Directory Tree' and using the directional keys to highlight the option). If you want to type the **DIR \DOS** command, select the 'Command Prompt' option from the 'Main' menu of DOS Shell.

Amongst the many files to be listed will be the ones shown below, the size and creation dates of which are dependent on the version of MS-DOS you are running on your computer. The ones shown below are related to MS-DOS version 5.

Filename	Extension	Size	Date	Time
APPEND	EXE	10774	09/04/91	5:00
BACKUP	EXE	36092	09/06/91	5:00
CHKDSK	EXE	16200	09/06/91	5:00
COMMAND	COM	47845	09/04/91	5:00
CONFIG	SYS	252	22/10/91	5:00
COUNTRY	SYS	17069	09/04/91	5:00
DISKCOPY	COM	11793	09/04/91	5:00
EDIT	COM	413	09/04/91	5:00
FORMAT	COM	32911	09/04/91	5:00
KEYBOARD	SYS	34697	09/04/91	5:00
LABEL	EXE	9390	09/04/91	5:00
PRINT	EXE	15656	09/04/91	5:00
RESTORE	EXE	38294	09/04/91	5:00
SORT	EXE	6938	09/04/91	5:00
UNDELETE	EXE	13924	09/04/91	5:00
XCOPY	EXE	15804	09/04/91	5:00

Note that a filename consists of up to 8 alphanumeric characters (letters and numbers only) and has a three letter extension, separated from the filename by a period, i.e. COMMAND.COM or CONFIG.SYS, without any spaces in between, unlike the listing appearing on your screen, where the periods have been omitted (but not in a DOS Shell directory listing) and the extensions have been tabulated as above.

Some of these files might have different extensions from the ones shown above, i.e. BACKUP.EXE might appear as BACKUP.COM in your system, as the extensions tend to differ for different versions of MS-DOS. The size of each file (in bytes) is also given on the listing together with the date and time it was created, which again might differ for different versions. DOS Shell directory listings do not show the time.

The extensions .COM, .SYS and .EXE are the most common extensions of the files which make up MS-DOS. They contain instructions which are executed directly by the computer. Other extensions commonly used by programs or users are:

.BAK   .BAS   .BAT   .DAT   .DOC   TXT   .TMP

which indicate 'back-up' files, 'Basic' programs, 'batch' files, 'data' files, 'document' files, 'text' files and 'temporary' files, respectively.

Command Parameters, Switches & Filters:

Returning to the result of issuing the DIR command; what is more likely to have happened in your case (unless you are running the DOS Shell - to be discussed shortly) is that the listing of the first half of the files on your disc will have scrolled out of view. In all, there are approximately one hundred utility files on the DOS sub-directory and you can only see the last twenty or so. To stop the scrolling of a long directory, use the /P switch after the DIR command, as follows:

```
C>DIR \DOS /P
```

which will page the directory, displaying twenty files at a time. Alternatively, you could see all the files with the extension .COM sorted alphabetically by using the |SORT filter, as follows:

```
C>DIR \DOS\*.COM |SORT
```

where the wildcard character '*' stands for 'all' files.

Commands can be entered in either uppercase or lower-case letters, but you must provide a space between the command and its parameters. For example, to obtain a listing of all the .EXE files on the DOS directory in paged format, you can type

```
C>DIR \DOS\*.EXE /P
```

or

```
C>dir \dos\*.exe /p
```

but you must type one space between the R (or r) and the back-slash (\). The space between the E (or e) and the slash (/) is optional; its presence only serves to improve readability.

Had you not included a space after DIR in the above command, MS-DOS would have responded with its favoured error message,

```
Bad Command or file name
```

which does not tell you very much, except that MS-DOS does not understand you!

The wildcard character '*' can also be used as part of the filename. For example,

```
C>DIR \DOS\DOS*.*
```

will list all the files with all extensions on the DOS directory, starting with the three characters DOS, irrespective of the ending of the filenames. There are 9 such files in MS-DOS 5.

The full MS-DOS command should also specify which drive you want to access, if it does not refer to the currently logged drive. Thus, typing

```
C>DIR A:DOS*.*
```

will access the specified files on the A: drive.

A more precise wildcard is the query character '?' which can be substituted for a single character in a filename. For example, typing

```
C>DIR \DOS\DOS????.*
```

will list three files which happen to have only four letters following the letters DOS. Again, these files are only available under MS-DOS 5.

How to use parameters, switches and filters when running the DOS Shell, will be discussed in the following chapters.

2. THE DIRECTORY STRUCTURE

If you are using a system with normal capacity disc drives, then organizing the files you keep on discs is relatively straightforward. The usual method would be to keep similar applications on the same disc, so that one disc might contain files on word processing, another on spread sheets, and another on databases. MS-DOS keeps track of all such files by allocating space on each disc, called a directory, in which such information as the name of each file, its size, the date it was last amended, etc., is kept.

However, as you move up to systems with high-capacity disc drives (1.2 or 1.44 Mbyte floppies) and especially to systems with hard discs of 20, 40 or more Mbytes, the amount of information you can store on them increases so much, that unless you organize the way you keep your files on such discs, you could easily spend all of your time trying to find one.

The Directory Tree
MS-DOS can help you to organize your files on disc by providing a system of directories and sub-directories. The key to the MS-DOS system is the 'root' directory, indicated by the back-slash sign (\), which is the main directory under which a number of sub-directories can be created. In turn, each sub-directory can have its own sub-directories, as shown below.

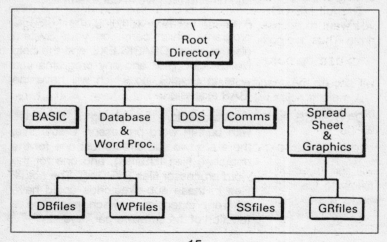

The root directory is shown here with five sub-directories under it, while two of these have their own sub-directories below them. For maximum efficiency, the root directory should contain only the System and start up files, together with information on its sub-directories, a kind of an index drawer to a filing system.

Files in different sub-directories can have the same name because MS-DOS can be told which is which via a system of PATH names. For example, a file in the SSFILES sub-directory could have the same name, say SALARY.TMP, as one in the GRFILES sub-directory. Nevertheless, we can instruct MS-DOS to fetch the file in the SSFILES sub-directory by giving its path name which is:

`\SPREADSH\SSFILES\SALARY.TMP`

whereas that of the file in the GRFILES sub-directory is:

`\SPREADSH\GRFILES\SALARY.TMP`

In the example shown previously, the contents of the various sub-directories might be as follows:

\	The root directory, containing the two hidden System files MSDOS.SYS and IO.SYS, the Command Processor COM-MAND.COM, the CONFIG.SYS file, the AUTOEXEC.BAT file, the names of all its sub-directories (five in our example).
BASIC	A sub-directory containing the QBASIC programs which came on your System disc, such as QBASIC.EXE and the help file QBASIC.HLP and any programs you write in QuickBasic which will have the .BAS extension.
DATABASE	A sub-directory containing a database with built-in word processor. Below this, there are two sub-directories; one for the database files (DBfiles), and one for the word processor files (WPfiles). The actual files in these sub-directories could have different extensions, which might be a function of the software package.

DOS	A sub-directory containing all the MS-DOS files comprising the external MS-DOS commands.
COMMS	A sub-directory containing communications programs, proprietary back-up software, etc.
SPREADSH	A sub-directory containing an integrated spreadsheet and graphics package. Below this, there are two sub-directories, one for the spread sheet files (SSfiles), and one for the graphics files (GRfiles). Again, the actual files in these could have different extensions which might be a function of the software package.

The Directory Listing

Were you to create the above directories with their sub-directories on your hard disc (you could, of course, set-up these on a floppy disc to avoid changing the configuration of your hard disc) and then type the command DIR, you would see the following display:

```
C>dir

    Volume in drive C is MS-DOS_5
    Directory of C:\

    COMMAND  COM     47845 09/04/91    5:00
    AUTOEXEC BAT       126 02/12/91   16:11
    CONFIG   SYS       125 02/12/91   16:11
    BASIC        <DIR>       05/01/92   10:53
    DATABASE     <DIR>       05/01/92   10:54
    DOS          <DIR>       05/01/92   10:54
    COMMS        <DIR>       05/01/92   10:54
    SPREADSH     <DIR>       05/01/92   10:54
            8 file(s)        48096 bytes
                          20431904 bytes free
```

The volume name (given above as MS-DOS_5) might be different in you case, as it depends on the label you gave your disc just after formatting. If you did not give a disc a label, then that line will read 'Volume in drive C has no label'.

17

The second line of the display depends on your system and you have no control over it. Note that directories are distinguished from files in the directory listing by the inclusion of the letters <DIR> (in angled brackets) against their name. The order of their appearance depends on the order of their creation.

These days, many program packages create their own directory structure during installation and suggest names for the required directories and sub-directories into which they deposit their files. What they don't do, is to create sub-directories for your data. These you must create yourself in order to avoid adding your data files into the same directory as the one holding the program files. Doing so, makes it easier for you to make a back-up of your data files onto floppy discs, and lays the foundation for a structured hard-disc system.

Using the DOS Shell

If during installation you chose the option of using the DOS Shell on start-up, or you type DOSSHELL at the C> prompt, then you will be able to see the directory tree which is displayed on the top-left part of the DOS Shell screen with a listing of the files of the logged directory (in this case the root directory) appearing on the top-right of the screen, as shown below.

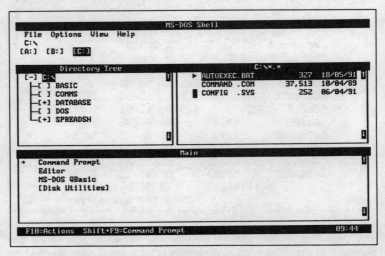

You can navigate around the DOS Shell screen, either by using the keyboard or by using a mouse.

18

To select an item with the keyboard, use the <Tab> key to move the cursor between screen areas, then use the vertical arrow keys to highlight the required item within the selected area and press <Enter>.

To select an item with the mouse, simply point to the required item and click the left mouse button. It is assumed, of course, that the required mouse driver is loaded according to the instructions that accompany the device. This requires you to include the command **MOUSE** within your AUTOEXEC.BAT file (more about this later).

The square to the left of the CONFIG.SYS file on the top-right area of the DOS Shell screen is the mouse pointer when DOS Shell is in text mode. If you have an EGA or VGA screen, then use the **Alt+O** command (press the **Alt** key and while holding it down, press the letter **O**) to reveal the pull-down **Options** menu and select the **Display** option, by using the down arrow key to highlight it and pressing <Enter>. A selection box appears in the middle of the screen, as follows:

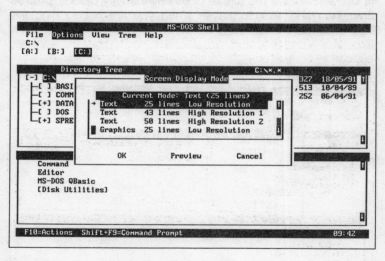

You can now select the **Graphics** option, which causes the DOS Shell to be redrawn on the screen, but this time in graphics mode, as shown on the next page. Note that the mouse pointer has now changed into an arrow, as displayed to the right of the CONFIG.SYS file.

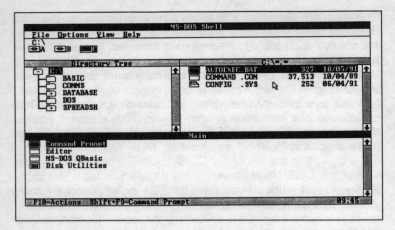

The same directory tree can be obtained by the use of the external MS-DOS command called 'tree' at the System prompt. Its use also allows you to see pictorially the way DOS structures directories and sub-directories when you are not running the DOS Shell, as shown below.

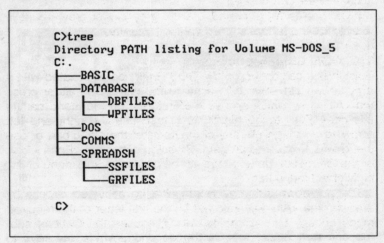

```
C>tree
Directory PATH listing for Volume MS-DOS_5
C:.
├──BASIC
├──DATABASE
│   ├───DBFILES
│   └───WPFILES
├──DOS
├──COMMS
└──SPREADSH
    ├───SSFILES
    └───GRFILES


C>
```

In previous versions of MS/PC-DOS, this command produced only a character listing of directories and sub-directories, as opposed to the current graphical visualisation which was introduced with the DOS version 4.0.

The topmost level in a disc directory structure is the root directory which is created automatically by MS-DOS when you format a new disc and, unlike other directories, it does not have a unique name. It is within the root directory that you can create additional directories and sub-directories and give them unique names.

When you create directories and sub-directories, MS-DOS creates what is known as the dot (.) and double dot (..) entries. These shorthand notations can be used to identify the current and the parent directory, respectively. Thus, typing

```
DIR ..
```

at the DOS System prompt, lists the files in the parent directory of the current sub-directory.

The two directory trees differ slightly in so far as the DOS Shell only shows first-level directories. Sub-directories with a plus sign (+) against their name in the directory tree, can be expanded by clicking on the plus sign. The sub-directories under the given directory will then be displayed and the plus sign changes to a minus sign (–). Clicking on the minus sign collapses the sub-directories.

If you don't have a mouse, use the grey <+> or grey <–> keys to expand and collapse a highlighted directory.

The DOS Shell Menu Bar

Each menu bar option on the DOS Shell has associated with it a pull-down sub-menu. To activate the menu bar, either press the <Alt> key, which causes the first item on the menu bar (in this case **File**) to be highlighted, then use the right and left arrow keys to highlight any of the items of the menu bar, or use the mouse to point to an item. Pressing either the <Enter> key, or the left mouse button, reveals the pull-down sub-menu of the highlighted menu item.

The pull-down sub-menus can also be activated directly by pressing the <Alt> key followed by the first letter of the required menu option. Thus pressing **Alt+O**, causes the Options sub-menu to be displayed. Use the up and down arrow keys to move the highlighted bar up and down within a sub-menu, or the right and left arrow keys to move along the options of the menu bar. Pressing the <Enter> key selects the highlighted option, while pressing the <Esc> key closes the menu system.

The Menu Bar Options:

Each item of the menu bar offers the options described below. However, dimmed or not visible command names indicate that these commands are unavailable at this time; you might need to select an item before you can use such commands. The biggest difference is observed with the **Files** sub-menu and it depends on whether you are working with files or programs (you have more options available to you with files).

You can display the information given below by selecting the DOS Shell **Help, Commands** option which causes a File List and a Program List to appear on your screen. Choosing an item from this lists, by highlighting it and pressing <Enter>, or pointing at it and clicking the left mouse button, produces the information on the specific item. This same information is listed below which should make reference to it easier to access.

The File Menu with Files

When DOS Shell is first entered, or if you select an item from the File-list area, such as the AUTOEXEC.BAT file, and then choose **File**, the following menu is displayed:

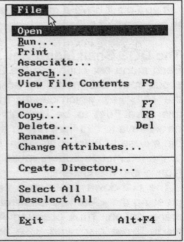

Open: Starts a selected program and an associated file, if there is one.

Run: Displays a dialogue box in which you type the name of the program file that starts the program.

Print: Prints the selected text file(s). The Print command only works if you have run PRINT.COM at the command prompt.

Associate: Associates all files having the same extension with a program, or a selected file with a program so that starting the program loads automatically the specified file.

Search: Finds files on all or part of the currently selected disc drive.

View File Contents: Displays the contents of the selected text file or binary file.

Move: Moves the selected file(s) from one directory to a directory you specify.

Copy: Copies one or more files in one directory to a directory you specify.

Delete: Deletes selected files or directories.

Rename: Renames a selected file or directory to the name you specify.

Change Attributes: Displays the attributes assigned to a file, such as Hidden, System, Archive, and Read-Only. Use this command to change these attributes.

Create Directory: Creates a new directory on the current drive. If a directory is selected, it creates a sub-directory within that directory.

Select All: Selects all files in the currently selected directory.

Deselect All: Cancels all selections except one in the currently selected directory.

Exit: Quits DOS Shell and returns to the system prompt.

The File Menu with Programs

If you select an item from the Program-list area of the Main group of programs, such as the **Editor**, and then choose **File,** the following menu is displayed:

New: Adds a new group or program item to the currently selected group.

Open: Starts a program and an associated file (if any), or displays the contents of a group.

Copy: Copies a program item to the group you specify. After chosing the command, open the group you want to copy to, and then press **F2**.

Delete: Deletes the selected group or program item from a group. Before deleting a group, you must delete all of its program items.

Properties: Specifies for a program item, the title, the command that starts the program, the start-up directory for the program to use, an application shortcut key, Help text, a password, and other properties.

Reorder: Moves the selected program item or group from its current location to the location you specify.

Run: Displays a dialogue box in which you type the name of the program file that starts the program.

Exit: Quits DOS Shell and returns to the system prompt.

Options Menu:

Selecting **Options** when working with either files or programs, displays the following pull-down menu:

Confirmation: Specifies if DOS Shell should prompt you for confirmation before deleting files or replacing files with duplicate names.

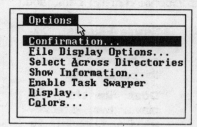

File Display Options: Lists files in sequence by name, extension, date, size, or order on disc. Also controls the display of Hidden or System files.

Select Across Directories: Controls whether or not you can select files in more than one directory. A mark next to the command indicates that it is active.

Show Information: Displays information on the selected file(s), directory and disc.

Enable Task Swapper: Turns on or off task swapping and displays the Active Task List to the right of the Program List. With it on, you can have more than one program open at a time and switch between them. A mark next to the command indicates that it is on.

Display: Changes screen mode and the resolution used to display DOS Shell.

Colors: Changes the colour scheme used for DOS Shell.

View Menu:

Selecting **View** when working with either files or programs, displays the following pull-down menu, but with files there an additional 'Refresh' command:

Single File List: Displays a single directory tree and file list for the current drive.

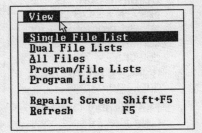

Dual File List: Displays two directory trees and file lists for the selected drive(s) in the file list.

All Files: Lists every file on the current drive, as well as information about the drive, its directories, and its files.

Program/File Lists: Causes the display of a list of directories and files and a list of groups and programs.

Program List: Displays a list of groups and program items in the current group.

Paint Screen: Redraws the screen, but does not update the list of files. For the latter to happen, use the 'Refresh' command.

Refresh: Re-reads the disc and updates the list to show changes caused by such actions as deleting or restoring files.

Tree Menu

This menu option is only available when you are working with files. Selecting **Tree** displays the following pull-down menu.

Expand One Level: Displays the next level of sub-directories for the selected directory in the Directory tree.

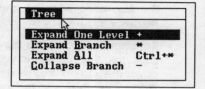

Expand Branch: Displays all levels of sub-directories in the selected directory in the Directory Tree.

Expand All: Displays all sub-directories in the Directory Tree.

Collapse Branch: Hides all currently displayed sub-directories in the selected directory in the Directory Tree.

Help Menu

Selecting **Help** when working with either files or programs, displays the following pull-down menu:

Index: Displays the DOS Shell Help Index.

Keyboard: Displays a list of shortcut keys you can use with DOS Shell.

Shell Basics: Displays a list of topics for basic skills you need to work with DOS Shell.

Commands: Displays a list of all DOS Shell commands, grouped by menu.

Procedures: Displays a list of topics you can look at for help on DOS Shell tasks.

Using Help: Displays a list of topics which explain how to use DOS Shell Help.

File Selection in DOS Shell:
To select a single file or multiple files while in DOS Shell, use either the mouse or the keyboard. The procedure is as follows:

- To select a single file: With the mouse click the name of the file, while with the keyboard use the arrow keys to highlight it.

- To select two or more contiguous files: With the mouse click the first filename you want to select, then press down the <Shift> key while you click the last filename of the block, while with the keyboard use the arrow keys to highlight the first filename in the list then press down the <Shift> key and while holding it down use the arrow keys to highlight the block of filenames.

- To select two or more non-contiguous files: With the mouse press and hold down the <Ctrl> key while you click at the required filenames, while with the keyboard select the first filename then press <Shift>+**F8** and move to the next filename, press the <Spacebar> to select the highlighted filename, go the next filename and press <Spacebar>, and so on, until you have finished when you press <Shift>+**F8**.

Managing Directories

To manage directories you need to be able to create them, select them, and delete them. These three tasks can be carried out easily from within DOS Shell.

To create a sub-directory, first select the directory under which you intend to create it, then use the **File, Create Directory** command and type its name on the displayed dialogue box which appears on the screen, as shown on the next page.

To change the selected directory, simply point to the required directory and click. With the keyboard use the arrow keys to highlight the desired directory.

To delete a directory, first select it, then use the **File, Delete** command to remove it, provided it is an empty directory. If not, you must first delete all the files within the unwanted directory, before you can delete it.

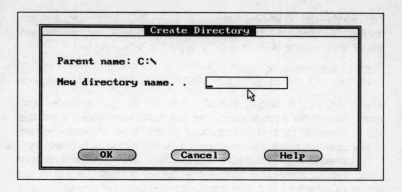

MS-DOS also provides three special commands which can be used at the system prompt for the creation and management of directories, in case you are not using DOS Shell. These are:

Command	Meaning	Example
MD	Make sub-directory	C>MD \BASIC
CD	Change directory	C>CD \BASIC
RD	Remove directory	C>RD \BASIC

However, before we explain these commands, make sure that your computer's prompt is of the form:

```
C:\>_
```

which indicates that the current directory is the root directory, shown by the back-slash (\). Having a prompt which indicates in which directory we are at any given time is extremely useful and prudent because without it we could be copying files to the wrong sub-directory without realising it.

The SETUP program of MS-DOS 5 should have inserted an entry into your AUTOEXEC.BAT file which produces this form of prompt. However, if this is not the case, because perhaps you are using an earlier version of DOS, then type

```
C>PROMPT $P$G
```

which on pressing <Enter>, changes the system prompt to the required form. This command should be included in your AUTOEXEC.BAT file (to be discussed later), but before you can do so, you will need to learn to use the **Edit** screen editor which will be explained in Chapter 4.

29

To create the sub-directory called BASIC from the system prompt, so that you can transfer to it all BASIC programs and files from the DOS sub-directory, type the following line

```
C:\>MD \BASIC
C:\>_
```

which makes the BASIC sub-directory in the root directory and waits for further commands. The full path was given after the MD command, by first specifying the root directory with the use of the back-slash (\), followed by the name of the sub-directory.

To transfer files from DOS subdirectory, first change directory using the CD command so that the logged directory is the target directory to which you will be copying the files, by typing

```
C:\>CD \BASIC
C:\BASIC>_
```

which causes the prompt to change, indicating that MS-DOS has actually changed directory. Without the prompt change, you would have had the typical 'where am I?' problem. Note that the moment we create a sub-directory we tend to refer to its parent as directory, even though itself might be a sub-directory to another parent directory.

To copy all BASIC programs and files from the \DOS directory to this new directory, type

```
C:\BASIC>COPY C:\DOS\QBAS*.*
```

Alternatively, we could have issued this command from the root directory without first changing directories. For example, the previous command would have to be typed as

```
C:\>COPY C:\DOS\QBAS*.* C:\BASIC
```

The first form of the COPY command says 'copy all files whose names start with QBAS from the \DOS directory to the logged directory', while the second form of the command says 'copy all files whose names start with QBASIC from the \DOS directory to the \BASIC directory.

30

Renaming Directories

Should you be dissatisfied with the name of an existing directory and you want to rename it, you can do so from within DOS Shell quite easily by selecting the directory you want to rename and then using the **File, Rename** command.

From the system prompt you will have to create another directory giving it your preferred name, copy to the newly created directory all the files from the unwanted directory, delete all files from the unwanted directory, and then remove the unwanted directory from its parent directory. This procedure is essential because:

(a) you can not rename directories from the system prompt,

(b) you can not remove directories unless they are empty.

As an example of the above procedure, let as assume that we have created, as discussed previously, a sub-directory to the root directory, called DATA. To have created such a sub-directory, we would have had to return to the root directory from whichever sub-directory we were at the time, by typing

```
CD \
```

at the prompt.

We now proceed to create a sub-directory to the DATA directory, called DOCS, by first changing directory from the root directory to that of DATA, as follows:

```
C:\>CD \DATA
C:\DATA>_
```

then make a sub-directory called DOCS by typing

```
C:\DATABASE>MD DOCS
```

at the prompt. Note that we have omitted the back-slash from in front of the sub-directory name which causes it to be made in the currently logged directory. Had we included the back-slash, the sub-directory DOCS would have been created as a sub-directory of the root directory.

Alternatively, we could make DOCS without first changing directory by issuing the MD command from the root directory, but giving the full path specification. Having made sub-directory DOCS, copy into it your files, as discussed previously.

Let us now assume that for some reason the directory name DOCS offends you and you would like to change it to WPDOCS instead. To do this you will have to type in the following commands, assuming you are at the root directory:

```
C:\>CD \DATA
C:\DATA>MD WPDOCS
C:\DATA>CD \DATA\WPDOCS
C:\DATA\WPDOCS>COPY \DATA\DOCS\*.*
C:\DATA\WPDOCS>CD \DATA\DOCS
C:\DATA\DOCS>DEL *.*
Are you sure? (Y/N)Y
C:\DATA\DOCS>CD \DATA
C:\DATA>RD DOCS
C:\DATA>_
```

In order of appearance, these commands do the following:

(a) change directory to DATA
(b) make a sub-directory called WPDOCS
(c) change directory to WPDOCS
(d) copy from sub-directory DOCS all files to the logged sub-directory
(e) change directory to DOCS
(f) delete all files from logged directory
(g) MS-DOS asks for confirmation
(h) change directory to DATA
(i) remove sub-directory DOCS.

Thus, re-structuring directories, moving files from one directory to another, or making back-ups of groups of files, is much easier with DOS Shell.

3. MANAGING DISC FILES

MS-DOS provides several commands which help you to manage your disc files efficiently. Some of these commands are internal and some are external. If the commands under discussion are external commands and your computer is a twin-floppy system, it will be pointed out to you so you can insert the System disc (the floppy disc on which you have installed MS-DOS with the use of the SETUP program) in the logged drive, which is the drive indicated by letter on the screen prompt.

The FORMAT Command

One of the first things you will need to do, as a new user, is to make a working copy of your system disc, or favoured software package, or just a back-up copy of your programs or data. Such packages and/or data are far too valuable in terms of money or time invested in producing them to be used continually without the safeguard of back-up copies.

Again, it is assumed that in the case of a hard disc-based system, your hard disc has already been formatted according to your manufacturer's instructions when setting up the system, and that all the MS-DOS external command files have been transferred onto it.

A new floppy disc must be formatted before it can be used by your computer's operating system. A floppy disc that has been formatted in one computer, can only be used in another computer if they are compatible and use the same operating system.

To format a disc, in the case of a hard disc-based system where the logged drive will be drive C:, insert the new floppy disc in the A: drive and type.

```
C:\>FORMAT A:/S/V
```

In the case of a twin-floppy based system, insert the system start-up disc in the A: drive, as FORMAT is an external command and needs to be loaded into RAM from the system disc, then insert the new floppy disc in the B: drive and type

```
A:\>FORMAT B:/S/V
```

Drive C: (or A: in the case of a floppy disc) is accessed momentarily, the FORMAT utility file is loaded into RAM and executed. You are then given instructions to insert a floppy disc in drive A: (or B: in the case of a twin-floppy disc system), and press <Enter> to begin. Be very careful never to format an already formatted disc (particularly the C: drive), as *all* files that might be on it will be lost.

The two switches, typed after the slash character (/), have the following meaning:

> The /s switch instructs MS-DOS to copy the two hidden system files and the COMMAND.COM file onto the newly formatted disc. This will be required if you intend to use the disc to boot up the system.
>
> The /v switch allows you to give a volume label to your new disc, after formatting is completed.

These and other available switches will be discussed shortly.

> DOS Shell => To format a floppy disc when using DOS Shell, use the **Disk Utilities, Format** command, as follows:

Select the **Disk Utilities** option from the Main group of programs, shown below:

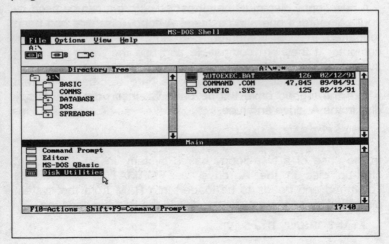

The selection can be achieved by double-clicking at the required option which causes the pull-down menu, shown below, to appear on the screen:

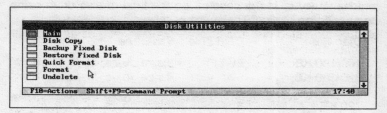

From this latter screen, double-click at the **Format** command, and follow the instruction given on the screen. The other options on the 'Disk Utilities' menu perform the following tasks:

Main: Returns you to the Main group of programs.

Disk Copy: Copies the contents of a floppy disc to another floppy disc.

Backup Fixed Disk: Copies files from the hard disc onto several consecutively numbered floppy discs.

Restore Fixed Disk: Restores files to the hard disc that were backed up onto floppies.

Quick Format: Re-formats already formatted discs by deleting the File Allocation Table (FAT) - more about this later.

Format: Formats new discs so they can be recognised by MS-DOS.

Undelete: Undeletes files. However, if your disc is full, using this program may render some deleted files unrecoverable.

The above disc utilities will be discussed and explained as and when the relevant commands are introduced in the book. They were listed above all together for convenience, as we were discussing the disc utilities available with DOS Shell.

Type and Size of Discs:

There are some additional switches that can be used with the FORMAT command (whether you are using DOS Shell or not) which, however, are dependent on the type of disc drive being used and size of disc. These are as follows:

Disc type	Disc size	Switches
160/180 KB	5¼"	/f:size, /b, /s, /u, /q, /1, /8, /4
320/360 KB	5¼"	/f:size, /b, /s, /u, /q, /1, /8, /4
1.2 MB	5¼"	/f:size, /b, /s, /u, /q, /4, /t, /n
720 KB/1.44 MB	3½"	/f:size, /b, /s, /u, /q, /t, /n
2.88 MB	3½"	/f:size, /b, /s, /u, /q.

where

/f:*size*   specifies the size of the floppy disc to format. This switch can be used instead of the /t and /n switches. Use one of the following values for size, which specifies the capacity of the disc in Kbytes:

160 / 180 for single-sided, double-density 5¼" discs,
320 / 360 for double-sided, double-density 5¼" discs,
720 for double-sided, double-density 3½" discs,
1200 for double-sided, high-capacity 5¼" discs,
1440 for double-sided, high-capacity 3½" discs,
2880 for 2.88 MB, double-sided, 3½" discs.

/b   reserves space for the system files IO.SYS and MSDOS.SYS on a newly formatted disc

/s   copies the operating system files IO.SYS, MSDOS.SYS, and COMMAND.COM from the system's start-up drive to the newly formatted disc

/u   specifies an unconditional format operation for a disc, which destroys all existing data on the disc and prevents you from later unformatting the disc

/q   deletes the file allocation table (FAT) and the root directory of a previously formatted disc, but does not scan the disc for bad sectors

/1   formats only one side of the disc (seldom used)

/8   formats 8 sectors per track (seldom used)

36

/4	formats 40 tracks with 9 sectors per track for 360 Kbytes using a 1.2 Mbyte high-capacity disc drive. This switch must be used if you are using double-density, but not high-capacity discs in a 1.2 Mbyte drive
/t	specifies the number of tracks, written as /t:40 for forty tracks. To format a 720 Kbytes double-sided disc in a high-capacity 3.5" disc drive (1.44 Mbytes), use switches t:80/n:9
/n	specifies the number of sectors per track to format, written as /n:9 for nine sectors.

Switches f:*size*, /b, /u, and /q, are new to MS-DOS 5, while switches /1, /4, and /8 are kept for backward compatibility to earlier versions of DOS. If switches /t or /n are specified, then both parameters must be entered. All other switches can be used separately or omitted altogether from the command. Omitting the /s switch from the FORMAT command saves disc space.

The SYS Command

Should you change your mind after you have formatted a disc without the use of the /s switch, you can use the external SYS command to transfer the system files from the system start-up drive onto a previously formatted disc, inserted in another drive. The command takes the form:

C:\>SYS A: in the case of a hard disc-based system, or

A:\>SYS B: in the case of a floppy disc-based system.

To successfully transfer the operating system to a disc with this method, the disc must either be newly formatted or else have space on it for the transfer of the operating system, by perhaps already having a different version of it on the target disc, or by having used the /u switch.

The order in which files are copied is: IO.SYS, MSDOS.SYS, and COMMAND.COM.

Differences Between Disc Drives:

The PC, XT and compatibles have 360 Kbyte double-sided, double-density disc drives. Discs are formatted with 40 tracks per side, 9 sectors per track with 0.5 Kbyte of information per sector, resulting in 360 Kbyte capacity.

The IBM AT, XT286 and compatibles have 1.2 Mbytes double-sided, high-capacity disc drives. Discs are formatted with 80 tracks per side, 15 sectors per track with 0.5 Kbyte of information per sector resulting in 1.2 Mbytes capacity. However, each track takes the same physical space as that of the 360 Kbyte drive, the difference being that the tracks are half the width of the 360 Kbyte drive.

Discs formatted on 1.2 Mbyte disc drives with the /4 switch use only one half of the width of each of the 40 tracks. This information can easily be read by a 360 Kbyte drive (as a result of tolerance in signal level), provided the other half of the track is completely clear. Should you now use the 360 Kbyte drive to write to the disc, information is written to the full width of the track which can still be read by the 1.2 Mbyte disc drive (again, as a result of tolerance in signal level). However, any subsequent writing to such a disc using the 1.2 Mbyte drive, results in changes to only one half of the track width. The result is half a track containing the new information with the corresponding other half of the same track containing the old, half-overwritten information, which makes it impossible for the 360 Kbyte disc drive to make any sense of it. Thus, to avoid such incompatibility between disc drives, always format double-density discs in a 360 Kbyte drive. Attempting to format a double-density disc to 1.2 Mbytes will result in many bad sectors with future loss of data becoming highly possible.

There are no such problems arising from the use of 3.5" discs which have been formatted as 720 Kbytes in a high-capacity (1.44 Mbytes) disc drive and subsequently used to read or write to them by either a 720 Kbyte or a 1.44 Mbyte disc drive. Again, avoid formatting non high-density discs to 1.44 Mbytes. If you do so accidentally, (this can happen if you use the DISKCOPY command with earlier versions of DOS to copy files from a 720 Kbytes disc to a high-capacity disc), do not attempt to re-format the high-capacity disc to 1.44 Mbytes, because the higher current used by the disc drive to format it to 720 Kbytes can not be wiped out by the re-formatting process.

The COPY Command

To copy all files on the disc in the logged drive to the disc in the A: drive, type

```
C:\>COPY *.* A:
```

Note the most useful three-character combination in MS-DOS, namely *.* which means 'all filenames with all extensions'.

However, if you wanted to copy a set of files from drive A: to drive C:, while being logged onto the C: drive, type

```
C:\>COPY A:*.DOC C:
```

which means 'copy from the A: drive all the files with extension .DOC to the C: drive'.

The /v switch can be used at the end of the COPY command to force MS-DOS to verify that the file(s) it has copied can be read. For example,

```
C:\>COPY \DOS\FORMAT.COM A:/V
```

will copy the formatting utility file FORMAT.COM from the \DOS directory of the logged drive to the A: drive and force verification that the file can be read.

> DOS Shell => To copy files when using DOS Shell, select the file(s) you want to copy, then use the **File, Copy** command.

To change the default selection of files when using DOS Shell, use the **Options, File Display Options** command. This displays the following dialogue box:

```
┌─────────────────────────────────────────────────────────┐
│              ▓ File Display Options ▓                     │
│  ┌──────────────────────────────────────────────────┐    │
│  │ Name:     ▓*.*▓_                                   │    │
│  │        ▷                                           │    │
│  │                                   Sort by:         │    │
│  │                                                    │    │
│  │  [ ] Display hidden/system files   ⦿ Name          │    │
│  │                                    ○ Extension     │    │
│  │                                    ○ Date          │    │
│  │  [ ] Descending order              ○ Size          │    │
│  │                                    ○ DiskOrder     │    │
│  │                                                    │    │
│  │   (   OK   )      ( Cancel )       (  Help  )      │    │
│  └──────────────────────────────────────────────────┘    │
└─────────────────────────────────────────────────────────┘
```

The DISKCOPY Command

Both the formatting and copying can be done in one go by using the DISKCOPY command, as follows:

```
C:\>DISKCOPY A: B:
```

which will copy all the files from the A: drive, to the B: drive and format the disk in the B: drive at the same time, if not already formatted.

However, if the disc in the B: drive is already formatted, but at different capacity to that in the A: drive, and you are using a lesser version of DOS than version 5.0, then the disc in the B: drive is re-formatted to the same capacity as that in the A: drive. This problem has been overcome with MS-DOS version 5.

You can not use the DISKCOPY command to copy files from a floppy disc to a hard disc, or to copy files between two floppy discs of different size (such as 3½" and 5¼" discs).

Note: Sometimes it is preferable to use the FORMAT and COPY commands than use the DISKCOPY command when copying all files from one disc to another. The reason is that bad sectors are frozen out when formatting a disc with the FORMAT command and the subsequent use of COPY, avoids these sectors. The DISKCOPY command on the other hand, seeks to make an identical copy (sector by sector) of the original disc which means that it attempts to write on bad sectors, if any, which might lead to an unsuccessful copy operation.

> DOS Shell => To copy all files from one disc to another when using DOS Shell, use the **Disk Copy** program in the Disk Utilities.

The DISKCOMP & COMP Commands

These two external utilities are mostly needed if you use the DISKCOPY command. The first one compares the contents of two discs, while the second one compares the contents of two files. The commands take the following form:

```
C:\>DISKCOMP A: B:
```
compares the discs in the A: and the B: drives, while

```
C:\>COMP A:MORE.COM
```
compares the file MORE.COM which is to be found on the discs in the C: and the A: drives.

The DELETE & UNDELETE Commands
Unwanted files on a disc can be deleted, as follows:

```
C:\>DEL EXAMPLE.TMP
```
deletes EXAMPLE.TMP on the C: drive

```
C:\>DEL A:EXAMPLE.TMP
```
deletes EXAMPLE.TMP on the A: drive

```
C:\>DEL *.*
```
deletes all files on the logged drive.

Luckily, the use of the DEL *.* command evokes the response

```
Are you sure? (Y/N)
```

which acts as a safety net. It is a good idea to always check what you are about to delete from your disc by first using the DIR command.

For example, say you intend to delete all the .TMP files from your disc. First use DIR *.TMP and if what is displayed on screen is what you want to delete, then type DEL and press the **F3** function key. This has the effect of displaying on the screen the last command you typed on the keyboard, minus the characters you typed prior to pressing the **F3** key. Thus, DEL replaces DIR and the use of **F3** displays the rest of the command. In this way you avoid making any mistakes by re-typing.

As you will, no doubt, use this command at some time or other, it will be prudent to copy both your AUTOEXEC.BAT and CONFIG.SYS files into your DOS directory. In this way you will have copies of these vital files away from harm's reach!

DOS Shell => To delete files when using DOS Shell, select the file(s) you want to delete, then use the **File, Delete** command.

41

With MS-DOS 5, you can use the UNDELETE command to recover undeleted files. To test this command, first make a copy of your AUTOEXEC.BAT file by typing:

```
C:\>COPY AUTOEXEC.BAT TEST
```

or using the **File, Copy** command from within DOS Shell. Then, use the **Delete** command to delete the file TEST.

To undelete a deleted file, type the command

```
C:\>UNDELETE TEST
```

at the C:\> prompt. This causes DOS to display the following information:

```
Directory: C:\
File specifications: TEST.*

    Deletion-tracking file not found

    MS-DOS directory contains 1 deleted files

Using the MS-DOS directory

    ?TEST              327 18/05/91 16:52 ... A Undelete (Y/N)?y

    Please type the first character for ?EST   . : t

File successfully undeleted
```

DOS Shell => To undelete a file when using DOS Shell, use
the **Disk Utilities, Undelete** command.

The pop-up dialogue box offers you the switch /**LIST** which, however, only causes DOS to list the files that can be undeleted without actually recovering them. The following three additional switches can be used to recover files:

/all   recovers deleted files without prompting for confirmation on each file

/dos   recovers files that are internally listed as deleted by DOS, prompting for confirmation on each file

/dt   recovers files listed in the deletion-tracking file produced by the **Mirror** command, prompting for confirmation on each file.

The RENAME Command

The REN command is used to rename files. As an example, let us assume that we want to rename a file on the disc in the logged drive from its current filename OLDFILE.DOC to the new filename NEWFILE.DOC. This can be done as follows:

```
C:\>REN OLDFILE.DOC NEWFILE.DOC
```

Note the importance of spaces after REN and in between the two file names. The command can be interpreted as:

```
Rename from filename1 to filename2
```

To rename a file on a disc in a disc drive other than the logged drive, the disc drive specification must also be included in the command, as follows:

```
C:\>REN A:OLDFILE.DOC NEWFILE.DOC
```

Note that, if you intend to rename a file and give it a filename that already exists on disc, you must first delete the unwanted file before renaming, otherwise MS-DOS will refuse to obey your command, informing you that the filename you have chosen already exists on disc.

> DOS Shell => To rename a file when using DOS Shell, select the file you want to rename, then use the **File, Rename** command.

The CHKDSK Command

This command checks a disc, reporting whether it is formatted as single or double sided, how many files are stored on the disc, how much space they take and how much space is still available. The command also checks the RAM, reporting on both the total memory available and the number of bytes still free. The command takes the form:

```
C:\>CHKDSK
```
which checks the disc in the logged drive, or

```
C:\>CHKDSK A:
```
which checks the disc in the A: drive.

The additional /f switch, allows CHKDSK to also do some routine maintenance, namely fixing lost clusters. A cluster is the minimum amount of space (one or more sectors) that can be allocated to a file on disc.

Each disc has a file allocation table (FAT) where a note is kept of which clusters have been allocated to which file. However, with heavy disc use, the file-allocation table can be corrupted and using CHKDSK will report 'lost clusters found'. The /f switch converts these into files and gives them the general name FILExxxx.CHK, where xxxx starts with 0000 and increments by 1. These files can then be checked and perhaps deleted if found to be useless.

The XCOPY Command

The XCOPY command allows us to copy files and directories, including lower level sub-directories, if they exist, to the specified destination drive and directory. The command takes the following form:

```
C:\>XCOPY source_filespec destination [switches]
```

where *source_filespec* specifies the source file or drive and directory you want to copy and *destination* can be the drive to which you want this source file to be copied to. For example,

```
C:\>XCOPY A:*.* B:
```

will copy all files in the A: drive to the B: drive. If you only have one floppy drive, you will be prompted to change discs.

Some of the *switches* available (for a full list see the 'Command Summary' section) are as follows:

/d   copies source files which were modified on or after a specified date

/p   prompts the user with '(Y/N?)' before copying files

/s   copies directories and their sub-directories unless they are empty

/v   causes verification of each file as it is written

XCOPY copies all files and sub-directories in the specified directory from one disc to another by reading from the source disc as many files as possible into memory, then copying them to the target disc. This is unlike the COPY command which copies each file in turn, therefore, taking much longer. However, when the target disc becomes full, XCOPY stops and does not ask for another disc to be inserted in the target drive. XCOPY can copy files even when the two discs are of different format, unlike the DISKCOPY command which requires that the source and target disc be the same format.

If you do not specify a path in the source filespec, XCOPY starts from the current directory. If you specify only a drive or path, but no files, XCOPY assumes you mean 'all files'. You can specify a target filename that is different from the source filename which causes files to be renamed while copying.

The BACKUP & RESTORE Commands

The external BACKUP command allows you to archive files from the hard disc. Since your disc contains valuable work, you must make additional copies of all your important files. The BACKUP utility allows you to generate those back-up copies on floppy discs. If you have a hard disc, you should use this utility often; daily or weekly, if necessary. The command takes the form:

BACKUP *source destination switches*

where   *source* is the drive/path/files to be backed up,
destination is the drive to back-up to, and
switches are:

/a to add the files to a disc in the destination drive

/d:*date* to back-up only files modified at or after the specified date

/f:*size* to cause the target disc to be formatted to a size which is different from the default size of the disc drive. Use one of the following values for size, which specifies the capacity of the disc in Kbytes:

160 / 180 for single-sided, double-density 5¼" discs,
320 / 360 for double-sided, double-density 5¼" discs,
720 for double-sided, double-density 3½" discs,
1200 for double-sided, high-capacity 5¼" discs,
1440 for double-sided, high-capacity 3½" discs,
2880 for 2.88 MB, double-sided, 3½" discs.

/m to back-up only files modified since they were last backed up

/s to also back-up sub-directories of the source path

/t: *time* to back-up only files modified at or after the specified time

/L: *filename* to create a log file, called *filename*, in which is stored a record of the current BACKUP operation.

Thus, to back-up, for the first time, all the word processor files whose path is \DATA\WPFILES, we type

```
C:\>BACKUP C:\DATA\WPFILES\*.* A:
```

while to back-up only files modified since they were last backed up, we type

```
C:\>BACKUP C:\DATA\WPFILES\*.* A:/M
```

In both cases, the wildcard characters *.* ensures that all files with all their extensions in the WPFILES sub-directory are backed up.

The RESTORE external command allows you to de-archive files. It is the only utility which can restore to the hard disc files previously copied to floppy discs using the BACKUP utility. The command takes the form:

RESTORE *source destination switches*

where   *source* is the drive to restore from,
destination is the drive/path/files to restore, and
switches are:

/a: *date* restores only those files last modified on or after the specified date

/b: *date* restores only those files last modified on or before the specified date

/p to prompt Y/N? before restoring, and

/s to also restore files from sub-directories.

Thus, typing

```
C:\>RESTORE A: C:\DATA\WPFILES\*.*/P
```

restores selected files from the floppy disc in the A: drive to the sub-directory WPFILES in the C: drive, provided these files were backed up from the same named sub-directories.

The PRINT & PRTSC Commands

The first time the PRINT command is used it has to be loaded into memory as it is an external MS-DOS command. However, from then on it resides in memory and can be used without having to re-load it.

The PRINT command provides background printing, that is, it can print long files while you are doing something else with your computer. In fact, using this command provides you with a print spooler which allows you to make and control a queue of several files for printing. The command takes the form:

```
C:\>PRINT filespec          adds filespec to print queue
C:\>PRINT filespec /C       cancels printing that file
C:\>PRINT /T                terminates all printing
C:\>PRINT                   displays files in queue
```

The PRINT command assumes that you have continuous paper in your printer. There is no facility to pause printing.

To print the two text files TEXT1.DOC and TEXT2.DOC, type

```
C:\>PRINT TEXT1.DOC
C:\>PRINT TEXT2.DOC
```

Wildcard characters can also be used in the command, as follows:

```
C:\>PRINT TEXT*.DOC
```

which will spool all the files starting with the characters TEXT and having the extension .DOC to the printer.

Text which is displayed on the screen can be sent to the printer by pressing the Print Screen (**Shift+PrtSc**) key.

On the other hand, pressing the **Ctrl** and **Print_Screen** keys simultaneously causes re-direction of output to the printer. To cancel the effect, repeat the same key stroke.

Managing Your System

MS-DOS provides several commands which help you to manage and control your system's environment. Some of these commands are internal MS-DOS commands and some are external. First we discuss the internal commands.

Changing the Access Date of a File:

If your computer is not fitted with a battery backed clock and you have not been entering the correct time and date on booting up the system, then all your saved files will be showing the default date 1/1/80 in the directory entry. To change this date for a given file, set the current TIME and DATE and type

```
C:\>COPY filespec + filespec
```

where filespec stands for drive, path, filename and extension. Ignore the message 'Content of destination file lost before copy' given by MS-DOS when this command has been executed.

The SET Command:

To find out what parameters have been set up, type

```
C:\>SET
```

at the prompt which would evoke the response

```
COMSPEC=C:\COMMAND.COM
PATH=C:\;C:DOS;C:\COMMS
PROMPT=$P$G
```

COMSPEC shows which Command Processor is being used by the system, while PATH and PROMPT display the corresponding commands in your AUTOEXEC.BAT file.

The TYPE Command:

This command allows you to see on screen the contents of text files. The command takes the form:

```
C:\>TYPE filespec
```

The TYPE command is useful because it only lets you have a look at the contents of files without changing the environment in any way. For example, if you ever wanted to find out what is held in either the CONFIG.SYS or AUTOEXEC.BAT files, then use this command rather than the editor; it is much faster.

48

If the text file you are looking at is longer than one screen full, then use **Ctrl+S** key sequence (while holding down the key marked **Ctrl**, press the **S** key once) to stop the scrolling of the display. Any key will start the display scrolling again.

Using TYPE on other than ASCII files (such as a .COM or .EXE file) could cause your system to 'hang' as a result of attempting to display certain sequence of machine code that might be contained in the file. If that happens, use the **Ctrl+Alt+Del** key sequence to re-boot the system.

In general, to use the TYPE command to see the contents of files, you must be logged into the sub-directory where the file is found or give the full filespec. For example, to look at the contents of the DOS.BAT file (which is to be found in the BATCH sub-directory) when at the C:\> prompt, you will have to use:

```
C:\>TYPE \BATCH\DOS.BAT
```

The TYPE command could be used to direct text files to the printer by typing

```
C:\>TYPE EXAMPLE.TXT >PRN
```

where PRN stands for 'printer' which is connected to the parallel printer port.

The VER & VOL Commands:
To find out which version of MS-DOS/PC-DOS you are currently using, type

```
C:\>VER
```

at the prompt.

To find out the volume label of the disc in the logged drive, type

```
C:\>VOL
```

at the prompt. If the disc was not labelled during formatting, then the computer will respond with

```
Volume in drive B has no label
```

otherwise the appropriate label will be displayed.

The MORE & SORT Filter Commands

The TYPE command can be used with a pipe (|) and the MORE external filter command, to view text files a page (23 lines) at a time - after displaying the first page, you are prompted to press a key to display the next page. As such, it can be combined with other commands to control scrolling of long ASCII files. For example,

```
C:\>TYPE EXAMPLE.TXT |MORE
```

or even used by itself (giving quicker response) as

```
C:\>MORE <EXAMPLE.TXT
```

can help you with viewing long text files if you are not used to or quick enough to use the **Ctrl+S** key sequence to halt scrolling, after issuing the TYPE command.

One of the ways in which the DIR command can be used with a pipe (|) and the the SORT external filter command, is to sort and display alphabetically the contents of a directory. For example,

```
C:\>DIR |SORT
```

will sort the contents of the logged directory, including the header and footer information, and display the result. For long directories, use this command together with the MORE filter, as follows:

```
C:\>DIR |SORT |MORE
```

to display the sorted directory a page at a time. A hard copy of the sorted directory of a disc could be obtained by typing

```
C:\>DIR |SORT >PRN
```

which re-directs output through the parallel printer port.

4. THE MS-DOS EDITOR

MS-DOS provides you with a full screen editor, called **Edit**, with which you can create special ASCII files that customise your system. These are text files which, when sent to the screen or printer, are interpreted as text, unlike the .COM or .EXE files which are binary files.

Edit can also be used to create the source code of various programming languages, such as Fortran and C. In such cases, do remember to give the files the appropriate extension, which for the two languages mentioned, are **.for** and **.c**, respectively.

To invoke **Edit**, the MS-DOS system start-up disc or a disc that contains it, must be accessible and the full path of the file you want to create or edit must be specified. Thus, typing the command:

```
C:\>edit test.txt
```

expects to find both **Edit** and the fictitious file **test.txt** on the disc in the logged drive (in this case C:), while typing

```
C:\>edit A:test.txt
```

expects to find **Edit** on the C: drive, and the file **test.txt** on the disc in the A: drive.

If the file does not exist on the specified disc or directory, then **Edit** displays a blank screen, as follows:

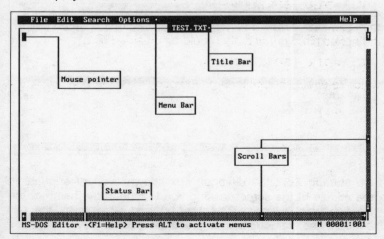

The **Edit** screen is subdivided into several areas which have the following function:

Area	Function
Menu bar	allows you to choose from several main menu options
Title bar	displays the name of the current file. If a new file, it displays the word <Untitled>
Status bar	displays the current file status and information regarding the present process
Scroll bar	allows you to scroll the screen with the use of the mouse.

The area bounded by the Title bar and the two Scroll bars is known as the view window. It is in this area that you enter the contents of a new file or load and view the contents of an old file.

The **Edit** screen can also be invoked from within DOS Shell by selecting the **Editor** from the Main group of programs, as shown below:

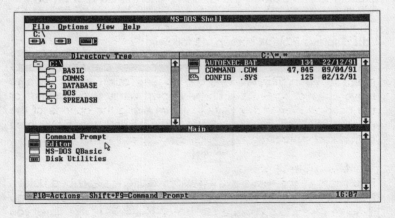

On starting **Edit**, the dialogue box shown overleaf appears in the middle of the screen asking you to type in the name of the file you want to edit. Type **test.txt** and either click the **OK** button in the dialogue box, or press the <Enter> key.

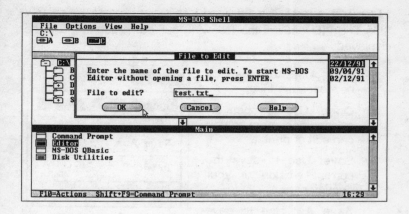

The Editor Menu Bar

Each menu bar option on the editor, has associated with it a pull-down sub-menu. To activate the menu bar, either press the <Alt> key, which causes the first item on the menu bar (in this case **File**) to be highlighted, then use the right and left arrow keys to highlight any of the items of the menu bar, or use the mouse to point to an item. Pressing either the <Enter> key, or the left mouse button, reveals the pull-down sub-menu of the highlighted menu item.

The pull-down sub-menus can also be activated directly by pressing the <Alt> key followed by the first letter of the required menu option. Thus pressing **Alt+O**, causes the Options sub-menu to be displayed. Use the up and down arrow keys to move the highlighted bar up and down within a sub-menu, or the right and left arrow keys to move along the options of the menu bar. Pressing the <Enter> key selects the highlighted option, while pressing the <Esc> key closes the menu system.

The Menu Bar Options:

Each item of the menu bar offers the options described below. However, dimmed command names in the **Edit** sub-menu indicate that these commands are unavailable at this time; you might need to select some text before you can use them.

The information given below can be displayed by highlighting the required sub-menu option and pressing the **F1** help key. This same information is listed overleaf for easier reference.

The File Sub-Menu

Selecting **File** causes the following pull-down sub-menu to be displayed:

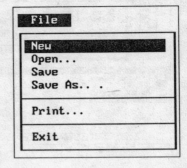

New: Use to create a new document file.

Open: Use to open an existing document so you can edit or print it.

Save: Use to save the current version of your document.

Save As: Use to save your document as a file. To preserve the previous version of your document, rename it in the File Name dialogue box.

Print: Use to print all or part of a document.

Exit: Use to quit the MS-DOS Editor environment.

The Edit Sub-Menu

Selecting **Edit** causes the following pull-down sub-menu to be displayed:

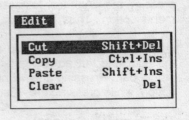

Cut: Use to remove selected text and put it on the Clipboard, a temporary holding area.

Copy: Use to copy selected text to the Clipboard. The original text remains unchanged.

Paste: Use to insert a block of text from the Clipboard at any point in a document.

Clear: Use to delete selected text without copying it to the Clipboard. The Clipboard's contents remain unchanged.

The Search Sub-Menu

Selecting **Search** causes the following pull-down sub-menu to be displayed:

Find: Use to search for a text string. You can request a case-sensitive match or a whole-word match.

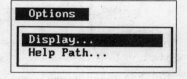

Repeat Last Find: Use to repeat the search performed by the most recent Find or Change command.

Change: Use to replace one text string with another.

The Options Sub-Menu:

Selecting **Options** causes the following pull-down sub-menu to be displayed:

Display: Use to control screen colour, scroll bars in windows, and the number of spaces the <Tab> key advances the cursor.

Help Path: Use to change the directories that the MS-DOS Editor searches to find the Help file EDIT.HLP

Help Menu

Selecting **Help** causes the following pull-down sub-menu to be displayed:

Getting Started: Use to find out about using MS-DOS Editor menus, commands, and dialogue boxes. Also to get Help on using the Editor and using options when starting the Editor.

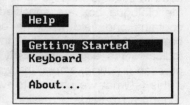

Keyboard: Use to find out about keystrokes for performing tasks on the MS-DOS Editor, and the WordStar keystrokes that can be used with the Editor.

About: Use to display the version number and copyright information for the MS-DOS Editor.

Dialogue Boxes:

Three periods after a sub-menu option, means that a dialogue box will open when the option is selected. A dialogue box is used for the insertion of additional information, such as the name of a file to be opened, or to be acted upon in some way.

To understand dialogue boxes, type the word 'hi' in the edit screen, then press **Alt+S**, and select the **Change** option from the revealed sub-menu of **Search**. The dialogue box shown below will now appear on the screen.

```
┌─────────────────────── Change ───────────────────────┐
│                                                       │
│  Find What: │hi                                     │ │
│             └─────────────────────────────────────┘ │
│                                                       │
│  Change To: │hello                                  │ │
│             └─────────────────────────────────────┘ │
│                                                       │
│                                                       │
│    [ ] Match Upper/Lowercase        [ ] Whole Word    │
│                                                       │
├───────────────────────────────────────────────────────┤
│ ◄ Find and Verify ► < Change All > < Cancel > < Help >│
└───────────────────────────────────────────────────────┘
```

The <Tab> key can be used to move the cursor from one field to another within a dialogue box, while the <Enter> key is only used to indicate that the options within the various fields within the dialogue box are specified correctly. Every dialogue box contains one field which is enclosed in emboldened angle-brackets (<Find and Verify>, in the above example). This field indicates the action that **Edit** will take if the <Enter> key is pressed (in our example, the word 'hi' will be changed to 'hello', if this is what we choose to type against the 'Find What' and 'Change To' fields. Pressing the <Esc> key aborts the menu option and returns you to the editor.

The cursor can be moved to any part of the text being typed in the view window, and corrections can be made, with the use of the key strokes described below.

Key	Function
Left Arrow	moves the cursor to the left by one character
Right Arrow	moves the cursor to the right by one character
Ctrl+Left Arrow	moves the cursor to the beginning of the previous word on the current line
Ctrl+Right Arrow	moves the cursor to the beginning of the next word on the current line
Home	moves the cursor to the first column of the current line
End	moves the cursor to the end of the last word on the current line
Up Arrow	moves the cursor up one line
Down Arrow	moves the cursor down one line
Ctrl+Home	moves the cursor to the first line of the current screen
Ctrl+End	moves the cursor to the last line of the current screen
PgUp	moves the cursor to the previous screen
PgDn	moves the cursor to the next screen
Ctrl+PgUp	moves the cursor left one screen
Ctrl+PgDn	moves the cursor right one screen
Ins	toggles the Insert mode from ON (its default position) to OFF and back again
Enter	moves the cursor to the beginning of the next line, provided the insert mode is in the ON position
Ctrl+Y	deletes the line at the current cursor position
Ctrl+N	inserts a blank line at the current cursor position
Shift+Arrows	marks block areas on the screen to be used with the sub-menu of the Edit option, namely Cut, Copy, Past, and Clear.

When areas of text are marked, with either the use of the **Shift+Arrows** or by clicking and dragging the mouse, **Edit** keeps the contents of a blocked (highlighted) area of text into a temporary storage area known as 'Clipboard' from which it can be retrieved later when the **Cut**, **Copy**, and **Paste** options are used. The Clipboard stores only one block of information at a time. If you attempt to store a second block of information, it simply overrides the previously stored block.

If you are not using a mouse, you might want to clear the scroll bars from the screen, to give you more room. This can be done by pressing **Alt+O**, selecting the **Display** option and pressing the <Tab> key until the cursor is positioned in the 'Scroll Bars' field. Pressing the spacebar toggles the option into the off position by clearing the letter X from within the square brackets.

If you are using a mouse, scrolling text in the view window is easy. Place the mouse pointer on the top, bottom, left or right of the scroll bars and click the left mouse button to scroll upwards, downwards, to the left or to the right, respectively.

There are a lot more commands associated with **Edit**, but you'll find that the ones given above are sufficient for almost all your needs.

Creating & Saving a Text file

As an example, type the following four lines in **Edit**'s view window:

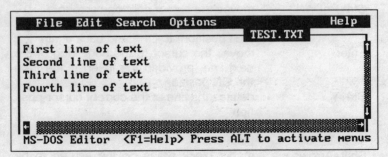

```
 File  Edit  Search  Options                      Help
                                    ┌─ TEST.TXT ─┐
┌──────────────────────────────────────────────────────┐
│First line of text                                    ↑│
│Second line of text                                    │
│Third line of text                                     │
│Fourth line of text                                    │
│                                                      ↓│
│←▓▓▓▓▓▓▓▓▓▓▓▓▓▓▓▓▓▓▓▓▓▓▓▓▓▓▓▓▓▓▓▓▓▓▓▓▓▓▓▓▓▓▓▓▓▓▓▓▓▓▓▓→│
└──────────────────────────────────────────────────────┘
 MS-DOS Editor  <F1=Help> Press ALT to activate menus
```

Editing Text:

To edit any part of the document, use the up or down arrow keys to place the cursor at the beginning of the line you want to edit, then use the right or left arrow keys to place the cursor at the required position where you want to begin editing.

If you have a mouse, simply point to the place you want to edit and click the left mouse button to place the cursor at the position occupied by the mouse pointer.

Use one of the above techniques to change the second line of our document to

```
Second line of text, edited
```

Selecting Text:
To select text, place the cursor at the required starting position, and while holding down the <Shift> key, press the right or left arrow keys to highlight as much of the text on that line as you like. With the mouse, place the mouse pointer at the required starting position and while holding down the left mouse button, move the mouse horizontally to the right or left to highlight the required text on that line.

If you try to select text which runs to more than one line, the whole line (first and subsequent) will be selected. Thus, you can either select text from part of a line, or you select text from whole lines.

As an example, select the words ' of text' (including the leading space) from the second line, as shown below:

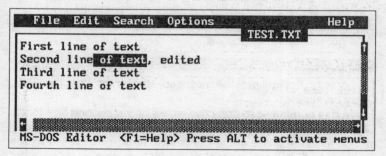

Moving Text:
Having selected the part of text you want to move, use the **Edit, Cut** command, then place the cursor at the required point where you would like to move the text to, and use the **Edit, Paste** command.

As an example, select the words ' of text' (including the leading space) from the second line, then use the **Edit, Cut**, followed by the **Edit, Paste** commands, to move the selected text to the end of the fourth line. The result is shown below:

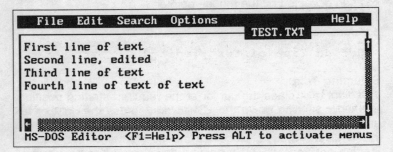

Clearing Text:
To remove text from a document without changing the contents of the Clipboard, highlight the unwanted text, then use the **Edit, Clear** command.

Use this command to remove from the fourth line both repetitions of the words 'of text', then, to prove that the contents of the Clipboard have not changed, use the **Edit, Paste** command to restore the fourth line to its original form.

In fact, you can paste the contents of the Clipboard to any part of a document, as many times as you like, because pasting does not empty the Clipboard.

Copying Text:
To copy text, highlight the required text, then use the **Edit, Copy** command.

Use this command to copy the whole of the second line to the Clipboard, then use the **Edit, Paste** command, to paste a copy of it on to the fifth line of the document. Next, change the words 'Second' to 'Fifth' and 'edited' to 'added', as shown on the next page.

You will have to use the <Del> key to delete the unwanted words as the editor is normally in 'insert' mode and when typing text it inserts it at the cursor position. To toggle the edit mode from 'insert' to 'overtype', press the <Ins> key once.

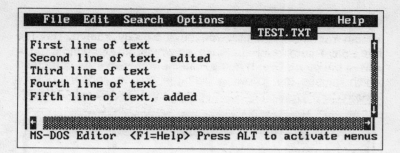

```
   File   Edit   Search   Options                    Help
 ┌─────────────────────────── TEST.TXT ───────────────┐
 │First line of text                                  ↑│
 │Second line of text, edited                          │
 │Third line of text                                   │
 │Fourth line of text                                  │
 │Fifth line of text, added                            │
 │                                                     │
 │←▓▓▓▓▓▓▓▓▓▓▓▓▓▓▓▓▓▓▓▓▓▓▓▓▓▓▓▓▓▓▓▓▓▓▓▓▓▓▓▓▓▓▓▓▓▓▓→│
  MS-DOS Editor   <F1=Help> Press ALT to activate menus
```

Finding Text:

To find a specific word or part of a word, use the **Search, Find**
command which causes the following dialogue box to appear
on your screen:

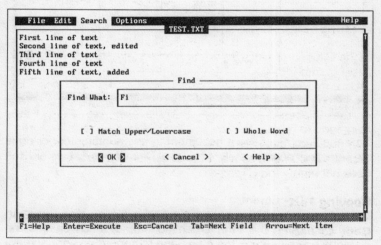

```
   File  Edit  Search  Options                              Help
 ┌──────────────────────── TEST.TXT ────────────────────────┐
 │First line of text                                        ↑│
 │Second line of text, edited                                │
 │Third line of text                                         │
 │Fourth line of text                                        │
 │Fifth line of text, added                                  │
 │          ┌───────────────── Find ─────────────────┐       │
 │          │                                         │       │
 │          │  Find What:  Fi                         │       │
 │          │                                         │       │
 │          │                                         │       │
 │          │  [ ] Match Upper/Lowercase   [ ] Whole Word │   │
 │          │                                         │       │
 │          │  ◄ OK ►      < Cancel >      < Help >    │       │
 │          └─────────────────────────────────────────┘       │
 │                                                            │
 │                                                            │
 │←▓▓▓▓▓▓▓▓▓▓▓▓▓▓▓▓▓▓▓▓▓▓▓▓▓▓▓▓▓▓▓▓▓▓▓▓▓▓▓▓▓▓▓▓▓▓▓▓→│
  F1=Help   Enter=Execute   Esc=Cancel   Tab=Next Field   Arrow=Next Item
```

Note that the word nearest to the cursor is offered in the 'Find
What' field as a default. In the above example, if the cursor is at
the beginning of the document, the default word will be 'First'.

As an example, to find all the words that begin with the letters
'Fi', after typing these in the 'Find What' field, press the <OK>
button. **Edit** highlights the first word containing these letters,
and to find the next occurrence you will have to use the **Search,
Repeat Last Find** command.

Saving a Document:

To save a document that you have already named, use the **File, Save** command. To save an unnamed document, or to save it under a different name, use the **File, Save As** command which causes the following dialogue box to appear on your screen:

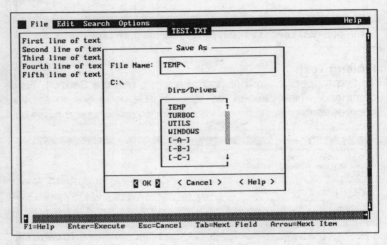

Note that you can save a document to any subdirectory or drive by selecting appropriately from the Dirs/Drives list within the dialogue box.

Opening a Document:

Once a document has been saved to a file on disc, you can open it by using the **File, Open** command which causes the dialogue box shown on the next page to appear on your screen.

Again, you can select any of the .TXT files (which is the default file extension) from the logged drive and subdirectory, or indeed change the extension to, say, .BAT if you want to work with batch files such as the AUTOEXEC.BAT file.

Also note that you can change the logged directory or drive by selecting appropriately from the Dirs/Drives list within the dialogue box.

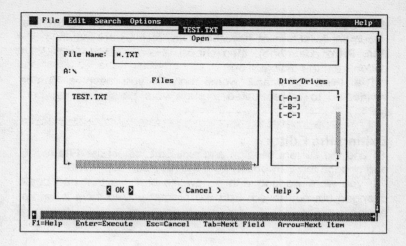

Printing a Document:

To print a document, use the **File, Print** command which causes the dialogue box, shown below, to appear on your screen:

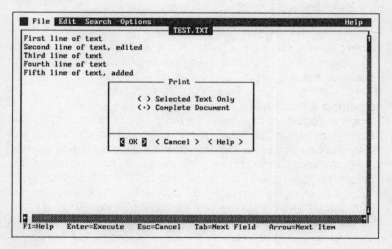

Note that you can choose to print the complete document (which is the default setting), or a pre-selected part of the document. If you are printing the whole document, simply press the <OK> button, but if you are printing a selected part of the document (which must have been selected before initiating the **File, Print** command), then choose the 'Selected Text Only' option from the dialogue box.

The **Print** command works only if you have a printer connected to or redirected through your parallel printer port (LPT1).

Exiting the Editor

To end the current session and exit **Edit**, select the **File** menu and choose the **Exit** option from the revealed sub-menu.

If you were working with a new file or a file that had been changed but not saved, **Edit** will prompt you to save it before exiting.

5. SYSTEM CONFIGURATION

The CONFIG.SYS File

This file allows you to configure your computer to your needs, as commands held in it are executed during booting up the system. The easiest way to amend this system file is with the use of **Edit**, as discussed in the previous chapter.

If you are setting up your system for the first time, you will need to change the CONFIG.SYS file that is created for you by the SETUP program, because it might not include all the commands you will require to run your system efficiently.

If your system had already been implemented with an earlier version of DOS, then the SETUP program will have added some extra commands to your CONFIG.SYS file. However, these additions are minimal and do not optimize your system, while others are not necessary and should be deleted.

If your system has been implemented by, say, your computer staff, do not edit this file or use **Edit** to look at its contents, unless you have to and you know precisely what you are doing, as the file contains entries that MS-DOS uses to define specific operating attributes. To view the contents of the file, use the **type** command at the system prompt.

DOS Shell => To view the contents of a file, select it, then use the **File, View File Contents** command.

The version of CONFIG.SYS shown below, was created by SETUP on installing MS-DOS 5.0 for the first time on floppies.

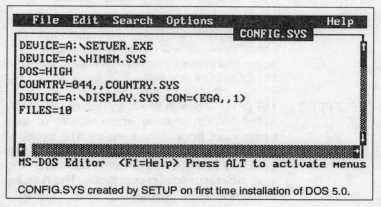

CONFIG.SYS created by SETUP on first time installation of DOS 5.0.

The version of CONFIG.SYS shown below, existed prior to upgrading to MS-DOS 5.0 from a previous version of DOS.

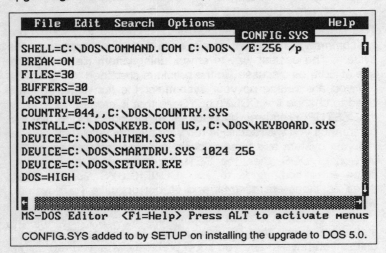

```
   File   Edit   Search   Options                    Help
                                     CONFIG.SYS
 SHELL=C:\DOS\COMMAND.COM C:\DOS\ /E:256 /p              ↑
 BREAK=ON
 FILES=30
 BUFFERS=30
 LASTDRIVE=E
 COUNTRY=044,,C:\DOS\COUNTRY.SYS
 INSTALL=C:\DOS\KEYB.COM US,,C:\DOS\KEYBOARD.SYS
 DEVICE=C:\DOS\HIMEM.SYS
 DEVICE=C:\DOS\SMARTDRV.SYS 1024 256
 DEVICE=C:\DOS\SETVER.EXE
 DOS=HIGH
                                                        ↓
 ←                                                      →
 MS-DOS Editor  <F1=Help> Press ALT to activate menus
```

CONFIG.SYS added to by SETUP on installing the upgrade to DOS 5.0.

The list below, contains commands that you can include within the CONFIG.SYS file. However, do remember that any changes made to this file only take effect after re-booting which can be achieved by pressing the 3 keys **Ctrl+Alt+Del** simultaneously.

Configuration Commands:
A brief explanation of the configuration commands, which can be included within the CONFIG.SYS file, is given below:

BREAK   By including the command BREAK=ON in the CONFIG.SYS file, you can use the key combination **Ctrl+C** (hold the key marked Ctrl down and press C) or **Ctrl+Break**, to interrupt MS-DOS I/O functions.

BUFFERS   MS-DOS allocates memory space in RAM, called buffers, to store whole sectors of data being read from disc, each of 512 bytes in size. If more data are required, MS-DOS first searches the buffers before searching the disc, which speeds up operations. The number of buffers can be changed by using:

BUFFERS=n

where n can be a number from 1 to 99.

However, as each buffer requires an additional 0.5 Kbyte of RAM, the number you should use is dependent on the relative size between the package you are using and your computer's RAM. Best results are obtained by choosing between 10-30 buffers.

COUNTRY   MS-DOS displays dates according to the US format which is month/day/year. To change this to day/month/year, use the command

COUNTRY=044

where 044 is for U.K. users.

Non U.K. users can substitute their international telephone country code for the 044. The default value is 001, for the USA.

DEVICE   MS-DOS includes its own standard device drivers which allow communication with your keyboard, screen and discs. However, these drivers can be extended to allow other devices to be connected by specifying them in the CONFIG.SYS file. Example of these are:

DEVICE=ANSI.SYS

which loads alternative screen and keyboard drivers for ANSI support - features of which are required by some commercial software.

DEVICE=SETVER.EXE

which sets the MS-DOS version number that MS-DOS version 5 reports to a program. You can use this command at the prompt to display the version table, which lists names of programs and the number of the MS-DOS version with which they are designed to run, or add a program that has not been updated to MS-DOS 5.

DEVICE=MOUSEAnn.SYS

allows the use of specific mouse devices.

DEVICE=VDISK.SYS n

allows you to specify the size n in Kbytes (default 64) of RAM to be used as an extra very fast virtual disc. With computers which have more than 640 Kbytes of RAM, the option /E can be used after n in the command to allocate the specified memory size from the extra area of RAM.

DEVICE=DRIVER.SYS

allows you to connect an external disc drive.

DEVICE=EGA.SYS

provides mouse support for EGA modes.

DEVICE=COMn.SYS

specifies asynchronous drivers for the serial ports, where for n=01 specifies an IBM PC AT COM device, and n=02 specifies an IBM PS/2 COM device.

DEVICEHIGH Loads device drivers into the upper memory area.

DOS Sets the area of RAM where MS-DOS will be located, and specifies whether to use the upper memory area. The command takes the form:

DOS=HIGH

DRIVPARM Sets characteristics of a disc drive.

FCBS Specifies the number of FCBs that can be opened concurrently. The command takes the following form:

FCBS=x,y

where x specifies the total number of files by FCBs, from 1 to 255, that can be opened at any one time (the default value being 4), and y specifies the number of opened files (from 1-255) that cannot be closed automatically by MS-DOS if an application tries to open more than x files.

FILES   MS-DOS normally allows 8 files to be opened at a time. However, some software such as relational databases, might require to refer to more files at any given time. To accommodate this, MS-DOS allows you to change this default value by using:

FILES=n

where n can be a number from 8 to the maximum required by your application which usually is 20, although the maximum allowable is 99.

INSTALL   This command runs a terminate-and-stay-resident (TSR) program, such as FASTOPEN, KEYB, NLSFUNC, or SHARE while MS-DOS reads the CONFIG.SYS file. The command takes the following form:

INSTALL=filespec[params]

where *params* specifies the optional line to pass to the *filespec* which must be FASTOPEN.EXE, KEYB.EXE, NLSFUNC.EXE or SHARE.EXE.

LASTDRIVE   This command is used if additional drives are to be connected to your system, or you are sharing a hard disc on a network. The command takes the form:

LASTDRIVE=x

where x is a letter from A to Z (default E).

REM   REM followed by any string, allows remarks to
                be entered in the CONFIG.SYS.

SHELL   Manufacturers of some micros provide a 'front
                end' or an alternative Command Processor to
                COMMAND.COM as real-mode command-line
                processor. To invoke this, the command
                SHELL must be included within the
                CONFIG.SYS file. The command takes the
                form:

                SHELL=FRONTEND.COM

                where FRONTEND is the name of the
                alternative Command Processor. The default
                value of SHELL is COMMAND.COM.

STACKS   Sets the amount of RAM that MS-DOS
                reserves for processing hardware interrupts.

SWITCHES   Specifies the use of conventional keyboard
                functions even though an enhanced keyboard
                is installed.

The COMMAND.COM Processor:
This command starts a new command processor that contains
all internal commands. This is loaded into memory in two parts:
the resident part and the transient part which can be overwritten
by some programs in which case the resident part can be used
to reload the transient part. The command takes the form:

   COMMAND [options]

with the following available options:

   /E specifies the environment size in bytes, with a default
       value of 160 bytes

   /P prohibits COMMAND.COM from exiting to a higher level

   /C executes a following command.

For example, the following statement

   C:\>COMMAND /C CHKDSK A:

which might appear in a program starts a new command processor under the current program, runs the CHKDSK command on the disc in the A: drive, and returns to the first command processor.

The AUTOEXEC.BAT File

This is a special batch file that MS-DOS looks for during the last stages of booting up and if it exists, the commands held in it will be executed. One such command is the KEYB xx which configures keyboards for the appropriate national standard, with xx indicating the country. For the U.K., the command becomes KEYB UK, and you will need to execute it if your keyboard is marked with the double quotes sign on the 2 key and/or the @ sign over the single quotes key and/or the £ sign over the 3 key.

The easiest way to amend this system file is with the use of **Edit**, as discussed earlier. If you are setting up your system for the first time, you will need to change the AUTOEXEC.BAT file that is created for you by the SETUP program, because it might not include all the commands you will require to run your system efficiently. If your system had already been implemented with an earlier version of DOS, then the SETUP program might have added some extra commands to your AUTOEXEC.BAT file during installation.

The version of AUTOEXEC.BAT shown below, was created by SETUP when MS-DOS 5.0 was installed for the first time on floppies.

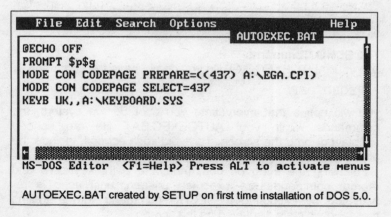

```
 File   Edit   Search   Options              Help
                                ┌─ AUTOEXEC.BAT ─┐
@ECHO OFF
PROMPT $p$g
MODE CON CODEPAGE PREPARE=((437) A:\EGA.CPI)
MODE CON CODEPAGE SELECT=437
KEYB UK,,A:\KEYBOARD.SYS




MS-DOS Editor   <F1=Help> Press ALT to activate menus
```

AUTOEXEC.BAT created by SETUP on first time installation of DOS 5.0.

The version of AUTOEXEC.BAT shown below, existed prior to upgrading to MS-DOS 5.0. No changes were made to this particular file by SETUP during installation on the hard disc.

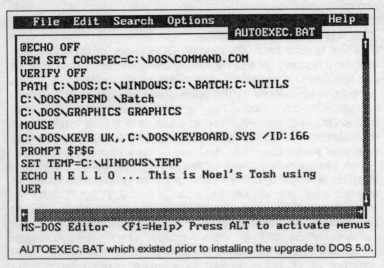

```
    File   Edit   Search   Options                        Help
                                              AUTOEXEC. BAT
 @ECHO OFF
 REM SET COMSPEC=C:\DOS\COMMAND.COM
 UERIFY OFF
 PATH C:\DOS;C:\WINDOWS;C:\BATCH;C:\UTILS
 C:\DOS\APPEND \Batch
 C:\DOS\GRAPHICS GRAPHICS
 MOUSE
 C:\DOS\KEYB UK,,C:\DOS\KEYBOARD.SYS /ID:166
 PROMPT $P$G
 SET TEMP=C:\WINDOWS\TEMP
 ECHO H E L L O ... This is Noel's Tosh using
 UER


 MS-DOS Editor   <F1=Help> Press ALT to activate menus
```

AUTOEXEC.BAT which existed prior to installing the upgrade to DOS 5.0.

Do remember, that any changes made to the AUTOEXEC.BAT file only take effect after typing

    autoexec

at the system prompt, or when re-booting the system by pressing the three keys **Ctrl+Alt+Del** simultaneously.

The ECHO Command:
If in your AUTOEXEC.BAT file you do not have the command

    @ECHO OFF

you will notice that every time you boot up the system, the commands within your AUTOEXEC.BAT file are echoed (displayed) onto the screen. To avoid such echoes, include the above command in your AUTOEXEC.BAT file.

Following the echo off command, the path, keyboard and prompt commands are executed unseen, until echo is re-activated by executing the ECHO command with a trailing message which is displayed on the screen.

72

The PATH Command:

It is most desirable to be able to use the MS-DOS external commands from anywhere within the directory tree without having to specify where the commands are kept (in this instance, we have transferred them into the DOS directory). The same could be said for the programs kept in the WINDOWS directory, the batch files kept in the BATCH directory, or the utility programs kept in the UTILS directory. This can be achieved by the use of the PATH command.

PATH can only find program files, that is, executable command files with the extension .EXE or .COM, or files that DOS recognises as containing such commands, as is the case with .BAT files; for data files you must use the APPEND command as is explained below.

Note the repeated reference to the C: drive within the PATH command, which allows the path to be correctly set even if the user logs onto a drive other than C:.

The APPEND Command:

It is conceivable that the software packages you will be using, require you to type a specific filename in order to activate them. However, some packages also include a second file (most likely a data file which might contain information about the screen display) which is loaded from the first when its name is typed.

In such a case, in addition to including the directory of the package in the PATH command within the AUTOEXEC file to point to the particular package, you must also include the name of the directory within the APPEND command, otherwise MS-DOS will search for the second (data) file in the root directory, as its extension will most likely be .SCR or .OVL and will not search for it down the PATH.

However, if the second file of a package is an executable file (a file with a .EXE or .COM extension), then you must use the /X switch after its name within the APPEND command.

In the display of the last AUTOEXEC file shown previously, the name of the BATCH directory was included in both the PATH and the APPEND command. This allows you to see the contents of a specific batch file, say those of DOS.BAT (to be discussed in the next chapter), by simply typing at the C:\> prompt:

```
TYPE dos.bat
```

If you do not include the BATCH directory in the APPEND command, MS-DOS will not be able to find the file, unless you specify its directory after the TYPE command. Yet when you type at the C:\> prompt:

    dos

MS-DOS searches down the path, finds the file, recognises it as being a file which contains MS-DOS commands (having the .BAT extension), and executes it.

The APPEND command must be included within the AUTOEXEC.BAT file in a position after the PATH command.

Other commands within the AUTOEXEC.BAT file carry out the following functions:

Command	Function
VERIFY	Turns on/off verification that files are written correctly to disc.
GRAPHICS	Allows MS-DOS to print on a graphics printer the information appearing on the screen. The parameter GRAPHICS indicates that printer is either an IBM Personal Graphics Printer, an IBM Proprinter, or an IBM Quietwriter printer.
MOUSE	Loads the mouse driver that comes with the mouse device.
KEYB	Identifies the type of keyboard connected to your system.
PROMPT	Changes the appearance of the MS-DOS command prompt. The parameter $P forces the display of the current drive and path, while the parameter &G displays the greater-than sign (>).
SET	Allows an environment variable named TEMP to be associated with the string C:\WINDOWS\TEMP. This is the subdirectory where Microsoft Windows creates and later deletes temporary files.
VER	Displays the version of MS-DOS running on your system.

A complete summary of all MS-DOS commands is given in the penultimate chapter of this book.

Optimising System Resources

To optimise your system so that resources are used most efficiently, involves choices between providing more memory for the programs you are running and increasing the speed of program execution.

As explained in Chapter 1 under 'Memory Management', your system can have three types of memory; conventional which is the first 640 Kbytes of RAM in which programs run, extended which is the memory above 1 Mbyte and is only available to systems with an 80286 or higher processor (the 384 Kbytes above the 640 Kbytes is referred to as the 'upper memory area'), and expanded which is the memory you install with memory boards.

To use extended memory efficiently, you must use the extended-memory manager HIMEM.SYS that comes with DOS 5 (and supersedes the version that comes with Microsoft Windows 3.0). As MS-DOS can run in extended memory, this can leave more conventional memory free for running other programs.

To use expanded memory, you must also use the expanded-memory manager that comes with the expanded memory board. Expanded memory is much slower than extended memory, so if you are thinking of installing more memory in your system, choose extended memory, particularly if you intend to use Microsoft Windows version 3.0 or later, as Windows works better with extended memory.

If, on the other hand, you have an 80386 or 80486 system with extended memory and you need to run programs that make use of expanded memory, then you can install the EMM386.EXE device driver that can use extended memory to provide expanded memory.

Increasing Conventional Memory:

To install HIMEM and run DOS in extended memory so as to free more conventional memory, use **Edit** and open your CONFIG.SYS file and add the following lines near the beginning of the file:

```
device=c:\dos\himem.sys
dos=high,umb
```

Following the above entries, the optimum order in which your CONFIG.SYS file should start device drivers is: (a) the expanded-memory manager if the system has actual physical expanded memory, (b) the EMM386 device driver which, however, must not be used if you are using an expanded-memory manager, (c) any device drivers that use extended memory, (d) any device drivers that use expanded memory, (e) any device drivers that you want to be loaded into high memory using the DEVICEHIGH command.

If you intend to use the EMM386 device driver to provide both expanded memory and to provide access to the unused portions of an 80386 or 80486 processor's upper memory area, use the **ram** switch, as follows:

```
device=c:\dos\emm386.exe ram
```

rather than the **noems** switch, as the latter switch prevents EMM386 from providing expanded memory, but is used to manage the upper memory area only. Although you can specify the size of expanded memory to be provided by including the amount in Kbytes prior to the **ram** switch, this could stop you from running Windows 3 in anything other than real mode. The reason is that EMM386 'converts' the equivalent amount of extended memory to expanded memory and the amount of extended memory left in your system might not be sufficient to run Windows 3 which in enhanced mode requires a clear 1,024 Kbytes of extended memory.

If you CONFIG.SYS file includes the **lastdrive** command and you are not using a network, set **lastdrive** to the letter E rather than Z, as each letter uses up about 100 bytes more than the preceding one. However, on systems with more than 1 Mbyte of memory, the saving that this provides is outweighed by the inflexibility introduced in not being able to use the **subst** command effectively, which associates a path with a drive letter.

Speeding up Your System:
To speed up program execution, use the **buffers** command in your CONFIG.SYS file to increase the number of buffers (up to 50, depending on the hard disc size) MS-DOS is using for file transfer. The more buffers the faster your system works, but it also uses more memory.

76

The most effective buffer sizes are: 20 for a hard-disc size of less than 40 Mbytes, 30 for a hard-disc drive between 40 and 79 Mbytes, 40 for a hard-disc drive between 80 and 119 Mbytes, and 50 for hard-disc drives in excess of 120 Mbytes. The command takes the form:

```
buffers=40
```

Another way of speeding up your system is to use the SMARTDrive disc-caching program and the RAMDrive memory-disc program in your CONFIG.SYS file. The appropriate commands are:

```
device=c:\dos\smartdrv.sys 1024 128
device=c:\dos\ramdrive.sys 512 /e
```

The first command specifies the cache size should be 1 Mbyte, but will not allow the amount of memory it is using to decrease below 128 Kbytes when Windows 3 requests extra memory to run an application. The second command allows you to use part of your system memory (512 Kbytes in this case), to emulate a very fast, but temporary disc drive which resides in extended RAM (specified by the switch /e). However, because information resides in RAM, it is lost unless you copy it onto the hard disc before you switch off your system. One possible use of a RAM drive is to use it as the TEMP environment variable so that programs who require to write temporary files to disc can use the RAM drive instead. To do this, use the following command within your AUTOEXEC.BAT file

```
set TEMP=d:\
```

and since such programs delete temporary files after use, you'll not have to worry about losing information. Use uppercase letters for TEMP as many programs do not recognise the environment variable if written in lower case.

Thus, taking into consideration all the points raised so far, your CONFIG.SYS file for a 386 processor could contain the commands shown on the next page.

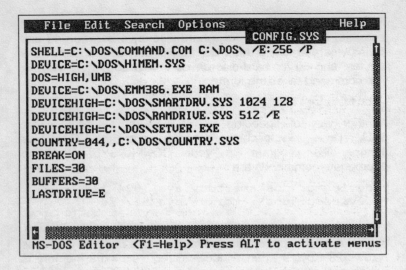

```
  File  Edit  Search  Options                         Help
                                   CONFIG.SYS
 SHELL=C:\DOS\COMMAND.COM C:\DOS\ /E:256 /P
 DEVICE=C:\DOS\HIMEM.SYS
 DOS=HIGH,UMB
 DEVICE=C:\DOS\EMM386.EXE RAM
 DEVICEHIGH=C:\DOS\SMARTDRV.SYS 1024 128
 DEVICEHIGH=C:\DOS\RAMDRIVE.SYS 512 /E
 DEVICEHIGH=C:\DOS\SETVER.EXE
 COUNTRY=044,,C:\DOS\COUNTRY.SYS
 BREAK=ON
 FILES=30
 BUFFERS=30
 LASTDRIVE=E



 MS-DOS Editor  <F1=Help> Press ALT to activate menus
```

When you have finish editing your CONFIG.SYS file, use the
File, Save command to save it.

The corresponding AUTOEXEC.BAT file, could contain the
following commands:

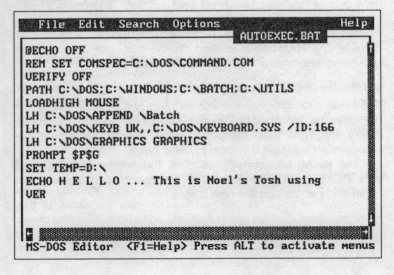

```
  File  Edit  Search  Options                         Help
                                   AUTOEXEC.BAT
 @ECHO OFF
 REM SET COMSPEC=C:\DOS\COMMAND.COM
 VERIFY OFF
 PATH C:\DOS;C:\WINDOWS;C:\BATCH;C:\UTILS
 LOADHIGH MOUSE
 LH C:\DOS\APPEND \Batch
 LH C:\DOS\KEYB UK,,C:\DOS\KEYBOARD.SYS /ID:166
 LH C:\DOS\GRAPHICS GRAPHICS
 PROMPT $P$G
 SET TEMP=D:\
 ECHO H E L L O ... This is Noel's Tosh using
 VER



 MS-DOS Editor  <F1=Help> Press ALT to activate menus
```

In the above AUTOEXEC.BAT file, all the memory-resident programs, such as **mouse**, **append**, **keyb**, and **graphics** are loaded into high memory with the **loadhigh** (you can abbreviate it to **lh**) command, while the **set** command is used to set the TEMP environment variable to the RAM drive D: created with the **ramdrive.sys** command within the CONFIG.SYS file (the program has created this RAM drive as drive D:, because this is the first available drive letter that is not assigned to an actual drive). Setting the TEMP variable to the RAM drive, should speed up programs that require to write temporary files to disc, as reading and writing to RAM is much faster that reading and writing to hard disc.

When you have finish editing your AUTOEXEC.BAT file, use the **File, Save** command to save it, then remember to reboot the system by pressing the three keys **Ctrl+Alt+Del** simultaneously.

The order in which the memory-resident programs were loaded into high memory, is of some importance. The basic principle is that you load the biggest program first, then check using the

```
mem /p
```

command, to find out whether a certain memory-resident program will fit into the available 'gaps'. You might find it useful to use the **|more** pipe at the end of the **mem** command to stop information from scrolling off your screen.

When MS-DOS encounters the **loadhigh** command, it attempts to load the specified program into the upper memory. However, if the program does not fit into one of the available upper memory blocks, DOS loads it into conventional memory instead. To find out where a particular program has been loaded, use the

```
mem /c |more
```

command.

Issuing this command, causes MS-DOS to display three columns of information; the first column lists the name of the program using your system's memory, the second column gives the size of the program in decimal, while the third column gives the size in hexadecimal. Both the contents of the Conventional Memory and the Upper Memory areas are listed.

If, however, you issue this command while running Windows 3 in enhanced mode (having first shelled out to the DOS prompt before issuing the command), or if you do not include the EMM386 device driver in your CONFIG.SYS file, then the **mem** command will not report the contents of Upper Memory.

If the name of a program or a device driver appears in the Conventional Memory area (apart from MSDOS, HIMEM, EMM386, and COMMAND), then the program or device driver is running in conventional memory, probably because it did not fit into the largest available UMB. This can happen if it is of the type that requires more memory when it is loaded than when it is running, or vice versa. Such a program or device driver might not fit into a UMB even if the size of its file is shown to be less than the largest UMB.

If programs do not load in high memory, then you might try including some additional information at the end of the line that loads the EMM386 device driver in your CONFIG.SYS file. This could take the form:

```
i=B000-B7FF i=E000-EFFF
```

which specifically informs the EMM386 memory manager that RAM is available between pairs of addresses (expressed with the i= option). You could also ask the EMM386 memory manager to specifically exclude segments of memory, by using the x= option. However, before you do any of this, install MS-DOS 5 on floppy discs, because if anything goes wrong, you will need a bootable disc to start up your computer.

Each machine has different regions of RAM installed between 640 Kbytes and 1024 Kbytes. For example, on a genuine IBM machines, the area of memory between E000-EFFF is the Basic language ROM. Also area C000-C7FF is available, whereas on compatible machines this area is probably not available because of the addressing of various devices such as disc controller firmware. Finally, on *any* machine with a VGA display adaptor, the area of memory used by the CGA system (B000-B7FF) is available to load programs in high memory.

To manage your processor's memory in the most efficient manner, if you are not willing to experiment, you could use one of several proprietary packages, such as Quarterdeck's QEMM386 version 6.01 or higher, which does all this for you automatically.

6. CONTROLLING YOUR SYSTEM

The DOSKEY Utility Program

MS-DOS 5 comes with an external utility called DOSKEY. This utility, when loaded into your system, allows you to recall the most recently entered DOS commands at the system prompt, for subsequent use, which can save you a lot of re-typing. You will find that learning to use DOSKEY will be extremely useful to you in what follows in this chapter.

DOSKEY is an example of a special type of program, called TSR (terminate-and-stay-resident). Once a TSR is loaded into memory, it stays in the background without interfering with the other programs you are running. To load DOSKEY into RAM, type

```
DOSKEY
```

at the system prompt and press <Enter>. This causes a message to appear on your screen informing you that the program has been loaded into memory.

If you are going to use DOSKEY frequently, it will be better to include the line

```
C:\DOS\DOSKEY
```

in your AUTOEXEC.BAT file, which loads the program automatically every time you switch on your system.

If you have a computer with an 80386 or higher processor, you should load DOSKEY in the upper memory with the command

```
LH C:\DOS\DOSKEY
```

so as to avoid occupying about 3 Kbytes of conventional memory.

Once DOSKEY is in memory, every time you type a command at the system prompt, the command is stored in the DOSKEY buffer which is 512 bytes long. To illustrate how this works, type the following commands, pressing <Enter> at the end of each line:

```
type config.sys
```

and after the contents of the CONFIG.SYS file have been displayed on screen, type

```
type autoexec.bat
```

and after the contents of the AUTOEXEC.BAT file have been displayed, type the commands

```
copy config.sys \batch
copy autoexec.bat \batch
```

The last two commands copy the two precious files into the \BATCH subdirectory, for safety's sake.

To recall the most recently executed DOS command, simply press the Up Arrow key. Each time this is pressed, the next most recently executed DOS command is displayed. In our case, pressing the Up Arrow key 4 times, takes us to the first command typed in the above example.

When the required command is displayed at the prompt, pressing the Left or Right Arrow keys allows you to edit the recalled command, while pressing <Enter> re-executes the chosen command.

The key movements associated with DOSKEY, are as follows:

Key	Result
Up Arrow	Displays the previous command in the buffer list.
Dn Arrow	Displays the next command in the buffer list.
F7	Displays a numbered list of the commands in the buffer.
F8	Cycles through the commands in the buffer that start with a letter you specify.
F9	Prompts you for the number of the stored command in the list (obtained by using the F7 function key).
PgUp	Displays the first command in the buffer list.
PgDn	Displays the last command in the buffer list.
Esc	Clears the command at the prompt.
Alt+F7	Clears the list of commands from the buffer.

Simple Batch Files

To complete the implementation of the hard disc, we need to create a few batch files which we will put in a sub-directory of the root directory, called BATCH. This will help to run the system efficiently. For example, we might require to know the exact name of a DOS or a COMMS command. This can be arranged by creating a batch file for each, to display the corresponding directory whenever the appropriate name is typed. As an example, first create the BATCH sub-directory, using the

```
C:\>MD \BATCH
```

command, then use **Edit** to create the DOS.BAT file in the BATCH sub-directory, as follows:

```
C:\>edit \BATCH\DOS.BAT
```

and type into the editor's screen the following information:

```
@ECHO OFF
CD \DOS
DIR /P
CD \
```

then save the file using the **File, Save** command. In line 2, the directory is changed to that of DOS and line 3 causes the contents of the DOS directory to be displayed using the paging (/P) option. Finally, line 4 returns the system back to the root directory.

However, before you can use the DOS.BAT batch file, you must include the sub-directory BATCH within the PATH command of your AUTOEXEC.BAT file. Having done this, save the changes and re-boot the system, so that the latest changes to your AUTOEXEC.BAT file can take effect. Now, typing DOS displays the DOS directory, while typing any external MS-DOS command, invokes the appropriate command. A similar batch file can be built for displaying the COMMS directory, the only difference being in line 2 of the file, so that the correct directory is accessed and displayed.

Using Replaceable Parameters:

After some time has elapsed and you have written several batch files using the

```
C:\>edit \BATCH\MYFILE.BAT
```

command, where MYFILE.BAT is the batch file you are writing, you might find it easier to write a special batch file which itself calls **edit**, tells it into which subdirectory you want it to be created, and also adds the extension .BAT automatically for you. To create this special batch file, use **edit**, as follows:

```
C:\>edit \BATCH\EDITBAT.BAT
```

and type into the editor's screen the following information:

```
@ECHO OFF
EDIT \BATCH\%1.BAT
CD \
```

then save the file using the **File, Save** command. Note the variable %1 in line 2 which can take the name of any batch file you might want to create. For example, typing

```
C:\>editbat MYFILE
```

at the prompt, starts executing the commands within the batch file EDITBAT.BAT, but substituting MYFILE for the %1 variable. Thus, line 2 causes entry into **Edit** and tells the editor that you want to create a file in the \BATCH directory, called MYFILE, with the extension .BAT added to it automatically.

As a second example, use the batch file EDITBAT.BAT, created above, to create a new batch file, which we will call ADIR.BAT, as follows:

```
C:\>editbat ADIR
```

and type the following instruction into the editor's screen:

```
@ECHO OFF
DIR \%1 |SORT |MORE
```

then use the **File, Save** command to save the file.

You can now use this batch file to display the contents of any directory listed in alphabetical order of filename, a page at a time, by simply typing **adir** *directory_name* at the prompt. For *directory_name* you could type **wp\docs** to have the contents of the **docs** subdirectory, of the **wp** directory, displayed.

84

Special Batch-file Commands

Apart from all the DOS commands, there are some specific commands which can only be used for batch file processing. These are:

Command	Action
CALL	Allows you to call one batch file from within another.
ECHO	Enables or disables the screen display of MS-DOS commands which are being executed from within a batch file, or displays the message that follows ECHO.
FOR	Repeats the specified MS-DOS command for each 'variable' in the specified 'set of items'. The general form of the command is:

FOR %%variable IN (set of items) DO *command*

where *command* can include any DOS command or a reference to the %%var. For example,

FOR %%X IN (F.OLD F.NEW) DO TYPE %%X

will display F.OLD followed by F.NEW

GOTO label	Transfers control to the line which contains the specified label. For example,

GOTO end

:end

sends program control to the :end label

IF	Allows conditional command execution. The general form of the command is:

IF [NOT] condition command

where 'condition' can be one of

85

EXIST filespec
string1==string2
ERRORLEVEL=n

Each of these can be made into a negative condition with the use of the NOT after the IF command.

PAUSE   Suspends execution of the batch file.

REM   Displays comments which follow the REM

SHIFT   Allows batch files to use more than 10 replaceable parameters in batch file processing. An example of this is as follows:

```
:begin
TYPE %1 | MORE
SHIFT
IF EXIST %1 GOTO begin
REM No more files
```

If we call this batch file SHOW.BAT, then we could look at several different files in succession by simply typing

```
SHOW file1 file2 file3
```

as the SHIFT command causes each to be taken in turn.

Combining Batch Files:
After you have created several batch files, one for each application you load onto your hard disc, plus several others to look at file lists in utility sub-directories you will realize that each such batch file takes up 2 or 4 Kbytes of disc space, depending on the cluster size of your hard disc, even though individual batch files might only be a few bytes in size. To remedy this situation, you could combine all your batch files into one batch file, call it LOAD.BAT, thus saving considerable disc space.

It will be assume here that you have 9 batch files which you would like to combine. These might be BATCH.BAT, DOS.BAT, and NORTON.BAT which produce a listing of the corresponding directories, QA.BAT which loads the Q&A integrated package of word processor and database, QPRO.BAT which loads the Quattro spreadsheet, TURBOC.BAT which loads the Turbo C language, SCALC5.BAT, LOTUS23.BAT and LOTUS31.BAT which load the spreadsheets SuperCalc5, Lotus 1-2-3 Release 2.3 and Lotus 1-2-3 Release 3.1, respectively.

Before we proceed with the writing of the combined batch file, we shall adapt the SHOW.BAT batch file discussed at the end of the previous section, so that we can obtain a listing on the printer of the contents of all the batch files we intend to combine into one, thus making our job easier. The new version of the SHOW.BAT batch file, which should be placed in the BATCH sub-directory, is given below.

```
@ECHO OFF
CD \BATCH
:begin
ECHO %1.bat
@ECHO OFF
TYPE %1.bat  |MORE >PRN
SHIFT
IF EXIST %1.bat GOTO begin
ECHO No more files
```

Thus, to obtain a listing of the batch files of interest, simply type

SHOW batch dos norton qa qpro turboc scalc lotus23 lotus31

and press <Enter>. Note that the SHOW batch file has been written in such a way as not to require the extension .BAT to be included after the entry of each of its substitution parameters.

Now, with the help of the listing of these batch files, you can proceed to write the contents of LOAD.BAT, as follows:

```
@ECHO OFF
IF %1==batch GOTO PL1
IF %1==dos GOTO PL2
IF %1==norton GOTO PL3
IF %1==qa GOTO PL4
IF %1==qpro GOTO PL5
IF %1==turboc GOTO PL6
IF %1==scalc GOTO PL7
IF %1==lotus23 GOTO PL8
IF %1==lotus31 GOTO PL9
GOTO END
```

87

```
:PL1 @echo off
cd\batch
cls
dir/p
GOTO END
:PL2
@echo off
cd\dos
dir/p
GOTO END
:PL3
@echo off
cd\norton
dir/p
GOTO END
:PL4
@echo off
cd\qa
qa
GOTO END
:PL5
@echo off
cd\qpro
q
GOTO END
:PL6
cd\turboc
tc
GOTO END
:PL7
cd\scalc5
sc5
GOTO END
:PL8
@echo off
cd\123r23
lotus
GOTO END
:PL9
@echo off
cd\123r31
lotus
:END
cd\
```

In the above batch file, we assume that you will be typing the entries corresponding to the substitution parameters in lower case. For example, typing

```
LOAD qpro
```

loads the Quattro Pro package.

If you want to make the batch file respond to both uppercase and lower-case letters, then each line containing the IF statement must be repeated, as shown below:

```
IF %1==qpro GOTO PL1
IF %1==QPRO GOTO PL1
```

and so on.

Adopting the lower-case option only, results in a batch file of 596 bytes, which replaces 9 batch files of 301 bytes of total size. However, by doing so you have saved 16 or 32 Kbytes of disc space, depending on the cluster size of your disc drive, which is a considerable saving.

Stopping Batch File Execution

To stop a batch file before all its statements and commands have been executed, press the two key combination

```
Ctrl+C
```

or

```
Ctrl+Break
```

more than once, if necessary. DOS displays a message asking you if you really want to terminate the batch file. Typing **Y** (for yes), terminates batch file execution.

If, on the other hand, you would like to temporarily stop a batch file, then either press

```
Ctrl+S
```

or the

```
PAUSE
```

key. This 'freezes' the screen until you press another key.

***

MS-DOS has many more commands which can be used to control a micro in special ways. However, this is an area which lies outside the scope of this book. What was covered here, together with the summary of the DOS commands given in the penultimate section of this book, is more than enough to allow effective control of a microcomputer.

If you would like to be able to write customised batch files, create specialist programs with the use of the **debug** program and learn how to design your own professional looking menu screens, then may I suggest that you refer to another book, entitled *A Concise Advanced User's Guide to MS-DOS (BP 264)*, also published by Bernard Babani (publishing) Ltd.

***

7. COMMAND SUMMARY

The following is a summary of the commands supported by the MS-DOS operating environment. For a fuller explanation of both commands and options, consult your system's PC/MS-DOS reference manual. The various commands are labelled internal or external, with external commands being accessible to the user only if the full filespec (drive and path) is given to where the appropriate command file resides.

Command	*Explanation*
append	External - sets a path that MS-DOS will search for data files when they are not in the current directory. It can even be told not to search already defined paths.
	Example: append c:\wproc\docs
	searches the \wproc\docs directory on drive c: for data files.
assign	External - assigns a drive letter to a different drive.
	Example: assign a=c
	allows all references to drive a: to go to the c: drive.
attrib [filespec]	External - sets or resets the *read only* attribute & archive bit of a file, and displays the attributes of a file.
	Switches:
	+r sets read-only mode of a file
	–r disables read-only mode
	+a sets the archive bit of a file
	–a clears the archive bit.
	Example: attrib +R filespec

| backup [filespec] | External - backs up one or more files from one disc to another. It can also automatically format the destination disc. |

Switches:

/a   adds files to be backed up to those already on the backup disc without erasing old files

/d   backs up only those files which were modified after that date

/l   makes a backup log entry in a file called BACKUP.LOG.

/f:*size*

causes the target disc to be formatted to a size which is different from the default size of the disc drive. Use one of the following values for size, which specifies the capacity of the disc in Kbytes:

160 / 180 for single-sided, double-density 5¼" discs,
320 / 360 for double-sided, double-density 5¼" discs,
720 for double-sided, double-density 3½" discs,
1200 for double-sided, high-capacity 5¼" discs,
1440 for double-sided, high-capacity 3½" discs,
2880 for 2.88 MB, double-sided, 3½" discs.

/m   includes files that have been changed since last backup

/s   backs up sub-directory files to file in current directory

/t:*time*

to back-up only files modified at or after the specified time

/L:*filename*

to create a log file, called *filename*, in which is stored a record of the current BACKUP operation.

Example: backup c:\ a:/s

backs up all files on the c: drive onto the a: drive.

break Internal - sets the Ctrl+Break or the Ctrl+C switch.

Example: break ON

cd (or chdir) Internal - changes the working directory to a different directory.

Example: cd\wproc\docs

chcp [nnn] Internal - selects current code page for as many devices as possible. Omitting *nnn* displays the current code page.

chkdsk [filespec] External - analyses the directories, files, and File Allocation Table on the logged or designated drive and produces a status report. It also reports the volume, serial number and disc allocation units.

Switches:

/f   fixes any problems found during the check
/v   causes the display of filespecs as they are being processed.

Example: chkdsk a:/f/v

93

cls	Internal - clears the screen.
command [filespec]	External - starts the command processor which is loaded into memory in two parts; the resident part and the transient part. If the transient part is overwritten by a program, it is reloaded.

Switches:

/e specifies the environment size in bytes (default = 160 bytes)
/p prohibits command.com from exiting to a higher level
/c executes a following command

Example: command /c chkdsk a:

starts a new command processor under the current program, runs the chkdsk command on the disc in the A: drive, and returns to the first command processor.

comp	External - compares two files and reports any differences.

Switches:

/a displays differences as characters
/c performs a comparison that is not case-sensitive
/d displays differences in decimal format
/l displays the number of the line on which differences occur
/n= compares the first specified number of lines of both files.

Example: comp file1 file2

copy [filespec]

Internal - copies one or more files to specified disc. If preferred, copies can be given different names.

Switches:

/a indicates an ASCII text file
/b indicates a binary file
/v causes the verification of data written on the destination disc.

Example: copy *.exe a:/v

copies all files with the .exe extension to the a: drive with verification.

ctty

Internal - changes the standard I/O console to an auxiliary (aux) console, and vice versa.

Example: ctty aux

moves all input/output from the current device (console) to an aux port such as another terminal. The command *ctty con* moves I/O back to the console.

date

Internal - enters or changes the current date.

debug

External - starts the debug program that allows you to create or edit executable files.

del [filespec]

Internal - deletes all files with the designated filespec.

Switch:

/p displays filenames to confirm deletion.

Example: del a:*.txt

deletes all .txt files from the a: drive.

dir [filespec]	Internal - lists the files in a directory.

Switches:

/p   displays the directory listing a page at a time

/w   displays the directory listing in wide format

/s   lists every occurrence, in the specified directory and all subdirectories, of the specified filename

/o: controls the sort order in which a directory listing is displayed. For example,

n   in alphabetical order

−n   in reverse alphabetical order

e   in alphabetical order by extension

−e   in reverse alphabetical order by extension

d   by date & time, earliest first

−d   by date & time, latest first

s   by size, smallest first

−s   by size, largest first

g   with directories grouped before files

−g   with directories grouped after files.

diskcomp	External - compares the contents of the disc in the source drive to the disc in the destination drive.
diskcopy	External - copies the contents of the disc in the source drive to the disc in the destination drive.

Switch:

/v   verifies correct copying.

doskey

External - starts the doskey program which recalls MS-DOS commands.

Switches:

/history   displays a list of all commands stored in memory. The switch can be used with the re-direction symbol (>) to redirect the list to a file

/macros   displays a list of all doskey macros. The switch can be used with the re-direction symbol (>) to redirect the list to a file

/bufsize=   allows the specification of the buffer size to be used for storing commands. The default size is 512 bytes, while the minimum buffer size is 256 bytes.

dosshell

External - activates the front-end graphical interface.

edit

External - activates the MS-DOS screen editor which is used to create or edit ASCII text files.

Switches:

/b   displays the editor in black and white

/g   uses the fastest screen updating for CGA displays

/h   displays the maximum number of lines possible for the monitor you are using.

edlin	External - activates the line editor edlin which can be used to create and edit ASCII text files.
EMM386	External - enables or disables expanded memory support on a computer with an 80386 or higher processor.
exe2bin	External - converts .exe files to binary format.
exit	Internal - exits the command processor and returns to a previous level.
expand	External - expands a compressed MS-DOS version 5 file.
fastopen [filespec]	External - store in memory the location of directories and recently opened files on a specified drive.

Switch:

/x allows use of expanded memory. If this switch is used, then the /x switch must also be used with the **buffers** command.

fc [filespec] External - compares two files and displays the differences between them.

Switches:

/a abbreviates the output of an ASCII comparison to only the first and last line of each set of differences
/b compares binary files
/c ignores the case of letters

/l	compares ASCII files line by line
/n	displays the line numbers during an ASCII comparison
/t	does not expand tabs to spaces
/w	compresses tabs and spaces during the comparison.

fdisk

External - sets up and partitions the fixed disc for use with MS-DOS and other operating systems. This command is also used to display and change the current active partition. It also supports an 80-column screen. It also has improved user-friendly commands to allow disc partitioning in megabytes or percentages instead of cylinders.

fdiskoff

External - could have another name, but its use is to park the fixed disc heads. This should be done before moving a computer equipped with a hard disc to prevent disc damage.

find [filespec]

External - searches for a specific string of text in a specified ASCII file or files.

Switches:

/v	displays all lines not containing the specified string
/c	prints the count of lines containing the string
/n	precedes each occurrence with the relative line number in the file
/i	search is insensitive to the case of letters.

Example: find "lost words" chap1

searches for the string *lost words* (which must appear within full quotes) in the named file (chap1).

format [filespec]

External - formats the disc in the specified drive.

Switches:

/8   formats with 8 sectors per track

/4   formats a double-sided disc with 40 tracks, 9 sectors per track for 360 KB in a high capacity (1.2 MB) disc drive per track

/n   specifies the number of sectors per track, i.e. /n:9 for nine sectors

/t   specifies the number of tracks, i.e. /t:40 for forty tracks

/s   copies the system files from the logged drive

/q   deletes the file allocation table (FAT) and the root directory of a previously formatted disc

/f:*size*

specifies the size of the disc to be formatted. Use one of the following values for size, which specifies the capacity of the disc in Kbytes:

160 / 180 for single-sided, double-density 5¼" discs,

320 / 360 for double-sided, double-density 5¼" discs,

720 for double-sided, double-density 3½" discs,

1200 for double-sided, high-capacity 5¼" discs,

100

1440 for double-sided, high-capacity 3½" discs,
2880 for 2.88 MB, double-sided, 3½" discs.

/v   allows a volume label to be given to the disc after the formatting process

/v:label
     allows you to specify *label* without prompting after the formatting process

Example: format a:/4/s

graftabl
     External - loads a custom designed, colour graphics font table into memory. It also supports the multilingual code page 850.

Switch:

/status
     identifies the code page selected for use by graftabl.

graphics
     External - it supports EGA and VGA graphics modes to provide screen dumps to IBM Graphics, Proprinters and compatibles.

Switches:

/r   prints the image as it appears on the screen (white characters on a black background, rather than reversed)

/b   prints the background in colour

/lcd   prints an image by using the liquid crystal display aspect ratio instead of the CGA aspect ratio.

help	External - provides online information about the MS-DOS commands.
install	External - it provides an improved method of loading memory-resident pop-up programs.
join	External - joins a disc drive to a specific path.

Switch:

/d   cancels any previous join commands for the specified drive.

keyb [xx]	External - selects a special keyboard layout. Omitting **xx** returns the current status of the keyboard.

Switches:

/e   specifies that an enhanced keyboard is installed
/id: specifies the keyboard in use.

label	External - creates or changes the volume identification label on a disc.
loadhigh (lh)	Internal - loads a program into the upper memory area.
md (or mkdir)	Internal - creates a new directory on the specified disc.
mem	External - it reports the amounts of conventional, expanded and extended memory that are available.

Switches:

/c   displays the status of programs loaded in conventional and upper memory area

/d	displays the status of currently loaded programs and of internal drivers
/p	displays the status of programs that are currently loaded into memory.
mirror	External - activates the mirror program which records information about one or more discs. The unformat and undelete commands use this information.

Switches:

/l	retains only the latest information about the disc.
/t:drive	loads a TSR (terminate-and-stay-resident) program that records information used by the undelete command to recover deleted files.

mode [options]	External - sets the mode of operation on a display monitor, parallel/serial printer or the RS232C port. The keyboard repetition and auto-repeat start delay time can be set. Also, it allows the setting of the number of rows to any of 25, 43 or 50 on the screen, and there is a wider range of serial-port configurations.

Options:

Display:	mode [n]
40	sets display width to 40 characters per line
80	sets display width to 80 characters per line

bw40	sets screen to black and white display with 40 characters
bw80	sets screen to black and white display with 80 characters
co40	sets screen to colour display with 40 characters
co80	sets screen to colour display with 80 characters
mono	sets screen to monochrome with 80 characters.

Printer: mode LPTi: [n][,[m][,p]]

i	sets printer number with legal values from 1 to 3
n	sets number of characters per line with legal values of 80 or 132
m	sets the number of lines per inch with legal values of 6 or 8
p	allows continuous re-entry on a time-out error.

Example: mode LPT1: 132,8

sets the printer in the first parallel port to 132 characters per line and 8 lines per inch.

Serial printer: mode LPTi: = COMj
This command redirects all output sent to one of the parallel printer ports to one of the serial (RS232C) ports. Before using this command, the serial port must be initialized using the *p* switch of the printer mode command.

i	sets printer number with legal values from 1 to 3

| | j | sets the serial port with legal values of 1 or 2. |

more   External - sends output to the console one screen-full at a time.

Example: type read.me | more

displays the contents of the read.me file one screen at a time.

nlsfunc   External - provides support for extended country information and allows the use of **chcp** command to select code pages for all devices defined as having code page switching support.

path   Internal - sets and displays the path to be searched by DOS for external commands or batch files.

Example: path c:\;c:\dos;c:\comms

will search the root directory as well as the dos and comms sub-directories for files with .COM, .EXE, and .BAT extensions.

print [filespec]   External - can be used to print text files in background mode, while other tasks are being performed. Using the command without options displays files already in the print queue.

Switches:

/d   specifies the print device such as PRN or AUX
/b   sets size of internal buffer with legal values from 512 to 16384 bytes, speeding up printing

/q	specifies the number of files in the print queue, normally 10, with legal values from 4 to 32
/t	allows cancellation of files in print queue
/c	allows cancellation of files in the print queue. It can be used with the /p switch
/p	allows the addition of files to the print queue. Both /c & /p can be used in the same command line.

| prompt | Internal - changes the command prompt. |

Example: pg

which allows the path of the current working directory to be displayed as the prompt.

| qbasic | External - activates the MS-DOS QBasic program that reads instructions written in the Basic computer language. |

Switches:

/b	displays QBasic in black and white
/g	provides the fastest update of a CGA monitor
/h	displays the maximum number of display lines possible for the type of monitor used
/editor	activates the MS-DOS screen editor
/run	runs the specified Basic program before displaying it.

rd (or rmdir)	Internal - removes the specified directory.
recover	External - recovers a file or an entire disc containing bad sectors.
ren (or rename)	Internal - changes the file name.

Example: ren a:\docs\mem1 mem2

will rename the mem1 file, which is to be found in sub-directory docs on a disc in the a: drive, to mem2.

replace [filespec]	External - allows easy updating of files from a source disc to a target disc of files having the same name.

Switches:

/a	adds new files that exist on the source disc but not on the target disc. You can not use this switch with the /s or /u switch
/p	prompts the user before replacing
/r	replaces read only files, as well as unprotected files
/s	searches all subdirectories of the destination directory and replaces matching files. You can not use the /s switch with the /a switch
/u	updates files with a time and date on the source disc more recent than those on the destination disc. You can not use the /u switch with the /a switch
/w	waits for you to insert a disc before replace begins to search for source files.

| restore [filespec] | External - restores one or more files that were backed up using the *backup* command. |

Switches:

/s	restores files in the specified directory and all files in any sub-directories of the specified directory
/p	prompts user before overwriting an existing file by restoring
/a:date	restores only those files last modified on or after the specified date. The date format varies according to the country setting in the CONFIG.SYS file
/b:date	restores only those files last modified on or before the specified date.
/e:time	restores only those files last modified on or before the specified time. The time format varies according to the country setting in the CONFIG.SYS file
/l:time	restores only those files last modified on or after the specified time.
/m	restores only those files modified since the last backup
/u	restores only those files that no longer exist on the destination disc
/d	displays a list of the files on the backup disc that match the names specified in *filename* without restoring any files.

set	Internal - sets strings into the command processor's environment. The general form of the command is:

set [name=[parameter]]

Set by itself displays the current environment.

setver	External - sets the MS-DOS version number that version 5 reports to a program.

share	External - installs file sharing and locking.

Switches:

/f: allocates file space, in bytes. The default value is 2048

/l: sets the number of files that can be locked at one time. The default is 20.

sort [filespec]	External - reads data from the console or a file, sorts it and sends it to the console or file.

Switches:

/r   sorts in reverse order

/+n   sorts the file according to the character in column n.

Example: dir | sort

sorts the output of the *dir* command in alphabetical order.

subst	External - allows substitution of a virtual drive for an existing drive and path.

Switch:

/d   deletes a virtual drive.

Example: subst d: a:\wproc\docs

will cause future reference to drive d: to be taken as replacement to the longer reference to a:\wproc\docs.

switches
External - it forces the conventional keyboard layout on to an enhanced keyboard.

sys
External - transfers the PC/MS-DOS system files from the logged drive to the disc in the specified drive. It also allows the specification of source drive and path commands to transfer system files across a network.

time
Internal - displays and sets the system time. It also supports a 12- or 24-hour format.

tree
External - displays the directory structure in graphical form.

Switches:

/f   displays the named of the files in each directory
/a   specifies that tree is to use text characters instead of graphic characters.

type
Internal - displays the contents of a file on the console.

undelete
External - restores files which were previously deleted with the del command.

Switches:

/list   lists deleted files that are available to be recovered

/all   recovers all deleted files without prompting

/dos   recovers only those files that are internally listed as deleted by MS-DOS, prompting for confirmation

/dt   recovers only the files listed in the delection-tracking file produced by the mirror command.

unformat   External - restores a disc erased by the format command or restructured by the recover command.

Switches:

/j   verifies that the file created by the mirror command has been saved and that it agrees with the listed information on the disc

/u   unformats a disc without using the mirror file

/l   when used with the /partn switch, lists every file and subdirectory found by unformat

/p   sends output messages to the printer connected to LPT1

/test   shows how unformat will re-create the information of the disc

/partn

        restores a corrupted partition table of a hard disc drive.

ver   Internal - displays the PC/MS-DOS version number.

verify   Internal - allows the verify switch to be turned ON or OFF.

Example: verify OFF

111

vol	Internal - displays the disc volume label, if it exists.
xcopy [filespec]	External - copies files and directories, including lower level sub-directories, if they exist, to the destination drive and directory.

Switches:

/a	copies source files that have their archive bit set
/d:	copies source files which were modified on or after a specified date
/e	copies sub-directories even if they are empty - use this switch in conjunction with /s
/m	copies archived files only, but also turns off the archive bit in the source file
/p	prompts the user with '(Y/N?)'
/s	copies directories and their sub-directories unless they are empty
/v	causes verification of each file as it is written
/w	displays a message before starting to copy.

8. GLOSSARY OF TERMS

ASCII	It is a binary code representation of a character set. The name stands for 'American Standard Code for Information Interchange'.
AUTOEXEC.BAT	A batch file containing commands which are automatically executed on booting up the system.
BACKUP	To make a back-up copy of a file or a disc for safekeeping.
BASIC	A high level programming language. The name stands for 'Beginner's All-purpose Symbolic Instruction Code'.
Batch file	An ASCII formatted file that contains MS-DOS commands which can be executed by the computer.
BIOS	The Basic Input/Output System. It allows the core of the operating system to communicate with the hardware.
Boot	To start up the computer and load the DOS operating system.
Booting up	The process of starting up the computer.
Branching	Transferring execution of commands to another part of a batch file.
Buffer	RAM memory allocated to store data being read from disc.
Byte	A grouping of binary digits (0 or 1) which represent information.
Cluster	A unit of one or more sectors. It is the minimum amount of space that can be allocated to a file on disc.
Click	To quickly press and release a mouse button.

Cold boot	The process of starting your PC by turning on the power switch.
COMMAND.COM	The Operating System's Command Processor which analyzes what is typed at the keyboard and causes execution of appropriate commands.
Command line	The line on the computer's screen into which you enter DOS commands.
Command Prompt	The prompt (C>) which appears on the computer's screen to let you know that MS-DOS is ready to receive a command.
CONFIG.SYS	A special file that allows the system to be configured closer to requirement.
CPU	The Central Processing Unit; the main chip that executes all instructions entered into a computer.
Cursor	The blinking line indicating where the next input can be entered.
Default	The command, device or option automatically chosen by the system.
Device driver	A special file that must be loaded into memory for DOS to be able to address a specific procedure or hardware device. These are normally installed from the CONFIG.SYS file at system start-up.
Device name	A logical name used by DOS to identify a device, such as LPT1 or COM1 for the parallel or serial printer.
Dialogue box	A box that MS-DOS displays on the screen when DOSSHELL is in operation, to ask the user for more information.
Directory	An area on disc where information relating to a group of files is kept.

Directory identifier	Displays the active disc drive and directory on the File System screen of DOS-SHELL.
Directory tree	A pictorial representation of your disc's structure.
Disc file	A collection of program code, or data, that is stored under a given name on a disc.
DOS	The Disc Operating System. A collection of small specialised programs that allow interaction between user and computer.
DOS prompt	The prompt displayed on the screen, such as A> or C>, indicating that DOS is ready to accept commands when not working with DOSSHELL.
DOSSHELL	The name of the front-end graphical interface provided by MS-DOS 5.
Double-click	To quickly press and release a mouse button twice.
DR-DOS	Digital Research's implementation of the Disc Operating System for compatible PCs.
Drag	To press and hold down the left mouse button while moving the mouse.
Drive name	The letter followed by a colon which identifies a floppy or hard disc drive.
Edit	The MS-DOS screen editor which is used to create and modify ASCII formatted files, such as batch files, and the CONFIG.SYS file.
Edlin	The MS-DOS line editor used in pre-DOS 5 versions of the operating system to create and modify ASCII formatted files.
Enter key	The key that must be pressed after entering data.

Expanded memory	This is memory outside the conventional RAM (0-640Kbytes) that DOS uses. It can be used by software to store data and run applications.
Extended memory	This is memory above the 1-megabyte memory address which DOS can use for limited operations.
External command	A command DOS executes by first loading it from an external disc file.
FAT	The File Allocation Table. An area on disc where information is kept on which space on disc has been allocated to which file.
File	The name given to an area on disc containing a program or data.
File list	A list of filenames contained in the active directory.
Filename	The name given to a file. It must not exceed 8 characters in length and can have an extension of up to 3 characters.
Filespec	File specification made up of drive, path, filename and a three letter extension.
Fixed disc	The hard disc.
Floppy disc	A flexible removable disc on which information can be stored magnetically.
Formatting	The process of preparing a disc so that it can store information. During formatting, sectors, tracks, a directory, and the FAT are created on the disc.
Function key	One of the series of 10 or 12 keys marked with the letter F and a numeral, used for specific operations.
GUI	A Graphical User Interface, such as that of DOSSHELL which uses visual displays to eliminate the need for typing commands.

Hard disc	A device built into the computer for holding programs and data. It is sometimes referred to as the fixed disc.
Hardware	The equipment that makes up a computer system, excluding the programs or software.
Hidden files	Files that do not normally appear in a directory listing, such as the IO.SYS and MSDOS.SYS files.
Internal command	One of a set of many command available to you at any time as they are loaded into memory every time you start your PC.
Key combination	When two or more keys are pressed simultaneously, such as Ctrl+Alt+Del.
Kilobyte	1024 bytes.
LABEL	The MS-DOS command which allows you to give a name to your disc.
Megabyte	1024 kilobytes.
Memory	Part of computer consisting of storage elements organised into addressable locations that can hold data and instructions.
Menu	A list of available options as appears in the DOSSHELL.
Menu bar	The horizontal bar that lists the names of menus.
Monitor	The display device connected to your PC.
Mouse	A device used to manipulate a pointer around your display and activate a certain process by pressing a button.
MS-DOS	Microsoft's implementation of the Disc Operating System for compatible PCs.
Operating System	A group of programs that translates your commands to the computer.

Parameter	Additional information appended to an MS-DOS command to indicate how the command should be executed.
PATH	The drive and directories that DOS should look in for files.
PC-DOS	IBM's implementation of the Disc Operating System for IBM PCs.
Peripheral	Any device attached to a PC.
Port	An input/output address through which your PC interacts with external devices.
Program	A set of instructions which cause the computer to perform certain tasks.
Prompt	The System prompt displayed on screen, such as A> or C>, indicating that DOS is ready to accept commands when not working with DOSSHELL.
RAM	Random Access Memory. The micro's volatile memory. Data held in it is lost when power is switched off.
Return key	The same as the Enter key.
ROM	Read Only Memory. The micro's non-volatile memory. Data are written into this memory at manufacture and are not affected by power loss.
Root directory	The main disc directory under which a number of sub-directories can be created.
Scroll bar	The bar that appears at the right side of the File List and Directory sections of the File System screen of DOSSHELL.
Sector	Disc space, normally 512 bytes long.
SHELL	A front end to MS-DOS or an alternative Command Processor.

Software	The programs and instructions that control your PC's functionality.
System	Short for computer system, implying a specific collection of hardware and software.
System disc	A disc containing MS-DOS' three main files and other Utilities.
System prompt	The prompt displayed on the screen, such as A> or C> indicating that DOS is ready to accept commands when not working with DOSSHELL.
Title bar	A horizontal bar across the top of each screen in DOSSHELL that contains the name of the screen.
Volume label	An identifying label written to a disc when a disc is first formatted.
Warm boot	The process of starting your PC with the use of the Ctrl+Alt+Del key combination.
Wildcard character	A character that can be included in a filename to indicate any character (?) or group of characters (*) that might match that position in other filenames.

INDEX

NOTES

NOTES

NOTES

NOTES